W0376902

Unterrichtsmodell

Series Editor: Hans Kröger

Echoes of the Empire – The Mixed Voices of a Colonial Past

20th Century English Short Stories

by Dr. Karola Schallhorn and Alexandra Peschel

Editor: Dr. Karola Schallhorn

Best.-Nr. 041223 1

Schöningh

EINFACH ENGLISCH

Vorwort

Der Titel der Reihe **EinFach Englisch** ist Ziel und Programm zugleich. Einerseits sollen Schülerinnen und Schülern literarische Zusammenhänge erklärt und ihnen damit der Zugang zu klassischen, aber auch neueren literarischen Werken erleichtert werden, und dies soll auf sprachlich einfache Art und Weise erfolgen, wodurch man der heutigen Schülergeneration sicherlich eher gerecht werden kann als mit schwierigen und komplexen Ansätzen. Andererseits sollen Lehrkräften erprobte und aus der Praxis stammende Unterrichtsmodelle angeboten werden, die ihnen einen raschen Zugriff auf unterschiedliche Materialien ermöglichen und einen Leitfaden für die Behandlung fiktionaler Texte oder die Analyse von Filmen im Unterricht bieten. Die Modelle können direkt und ohne Umschweife eingesetzt werden, langes Einlesen und eine zeitintensive Beschäftigung mit dem Stoff sind nicht erforderlich, wodurch die Arbeit, insbesondere die Unterrichtsvorbereitung von Lehrerinnen und Lehrern, erheblich erleichtert werden kann.
Schnell erhält man einen Überblick über **Figurenkonstellation** und **Inhalt** und kann sich problemlos entscheiden, ob ein Werk für eine bestimmte Reihe geeignet ist. Man weiß vorab, welche **Klausur** mit welchen Schwerpunkten geschrieben werden kann, und kann dieses bei der konkreten Planung eines Kursabschnittes entsprechend berücksichtigen. **Arbeitsblätter** sind als Kopiervorlagen gestaltet und **Tafelbilder** sind eingebettet in die **Leitfragen** zum eigentlichen Unterrichtsgeschehen, d. h., Material, das eingesetzt werden soll, befindet sich dort, wo es gebraucht wird; langes Suchen entfällt. **Piktogramme** geben optische Hilfen und Hinweise, sodass leicht zu erkennen ist, welche **Sozial-** bzw. **Arbeitsformen** sich bei den jeweiligen Aufgaben anbieten.
Die Unterrichtsmodelle basieren auf bewährten Verfahren der Textinterpretation und der Filmanalyse, dabei fließen neuere Erkenntnisse und Ansätze zu einer modernen Textrezeption angemessen ein. Der Umfang des Materials ist auf die tatsächlichen Gegebenheiten der Unterrichtspraxis abgestimmt und es sollte möglich sein, das Unterrichtsmodell vollständig und nicht nur in Auszügen im Rahmen einer Unterrichtsreihe einzusetzen. Das Prinzip der **„Components“** ermöglicht es darüber hinaus den Benutzern, unterschiedliche Reihen zu konzipieren, die an unterschiedlichen thematischen Schwerpunkten oder methodischen Fertigkeiten orientiert sind und ganz den individuellen oder kursspezifischen Bedürfnissen angepasst werden können. Dabei erheben die Unterrichtsmodelle nicht den Anspruch der Vollständigkeit, sondern eher den der Machbarkeit und Praxisnähe.

Das vorliegende Modell bezieht sich auf folgende Textausgabe und Audio-CD:

- **Textausgabe:** Echoes of the Empire – The Mixed Voices of a Colonial Past. Paderborn: Schöningh Verlag 2004; ISBN: 3-14-041224-X
- **Audio-CD:** Echoes of the Empire – The Mixed Voices of a Colonial Past. Paderborn: Schöningh Verlag 2004; ISBN: 3-14-062405-0

Arbeitsfrage

Audio-CD

Einzelarbeit

Partnerarbeit

Gruppenarbeit

Unterrichts-gespräch

Schreibauftrag

Hausaufgabe

Projektorientierung, offenes Unterrichtsangebot

Aufgaben mit kreativem Ansatz

Szenisches Spiel, Rollenspiel

Sprachliche Betreuung: Simone Duxbury-Ziemer

www.schoeningh.de
Schöningh Verlag, Jühenplatz 1–3, 33098 Paderborn

Druck A 5 4 3 2 1 / Jahr 2009 08 07 06 05
Alle Drucke der Serie A sind im Unterricht parallel verwendbar.
Die letzte Zahl bezeichnet das Jahr dieses Druckes.

Illustrationen: Reinhild Kassing, Kassel
Druck und Bindung: AZ Druck und Datentechnik GmbH/Kempten (Allgäu)

ISBN 3-14-041223-1

Who are the British?

Ask us, and you will find that we dance to
Music from America, Africa and Asia;
We eat food from Ireland, Italy and Jamaica;
We speak more than three-hundred languages
And we know over four-hundred different ways
To cook a potato. We look Celtic, Arab and Bengali;
We wear kilts, saris and football shorts; and if you get
Very close to us and look right into our eyes, you can
Almost see the history of the whole world.

Benjamin Zephaniah, We are Britain!, London, Frances Lincoln, 2003

Contents

Die Textsammlung *Echoes of the Empire – The Mixed Voices of a Colonial Past. 20th Century English Short Stories*

Die Textsammlung *Echoes of the Empire* lädt auf eine Zeitreise durch ausgewählte Kurzgeschichten renommierter Autorinnen und Autoren verschiedener ethnischer Herkunft ein. Der epochale Einfluss des britischen Empires und des Commonwealths und die damit begründete multikulturelle Gesellschaft in Großbritannien sowie die daher rührende neue „post-colonial“ oder „cross-cultural literature“ ist dabei Hintergrund und thematischer Schwerpunkt der Texte.

In den unter ***Component 1*** „Colonial Encounters“ zusammengestellten Geschichten begegnen die Leserinnen und Leser Ereignissen aus der Kolonialzeit. Hier werden sie mit menschlichen Extremsituationen konfrontiert, die die Absurdität und Brutalität des imperialistischen Systems eindringlich darstellen (**Joseph Conrad, *An Outpost of Progress*[1]; George Orwell, *Shooting an Elephant***) und die menschenverachtende Doppelmoral der Kolonialherrschaft anprangern (**W. Somerset Maugham, *The Force of Circumstance***).

Nachdem sich die kolonialherrschaftliche Verwaltung etabliert hat, beginnt die beiderseitige Akkulturation. Die Geschichten in ***Component 2*** „Cross-Cultural Experiences“ thematisieren den hierbei auftretenden „clash of cultures“ in den kolonialen Gebieten. Tabubrüche, Verstöße gegen Stammessitten, Verfall der tradierten Riten und Moral durch Unkenntnis der Sprache der Einheimischen oder durch bereits stattfindende Orientierung an der „weißen“ Zivilisation zeigen den Betroffenen ihre finanziellen und psychischen Grenzen auf (**Doris Lessing, *The Second Hut***), erzeugen tragikomische Situationen (**R. K. Narayan, *A Horse and Two Goats***) oder führen zum existenziellen Ruin (**Chinua Achebe, *Dead Men's Path*; Ngugi wa Thiong'o, *A Meeting in the Dark***).

In den *short stories* des ***Component 3*** „Postcolonial Consequences“ verändert sich die Perspektive. Am Ende des 20sten Jahrhunderts tritt in Großbritannien eine neue Generation von Schriftstellerinnen und Schriftstellern ins literarische Rampenlicht: mit **Muriel Spark, Qaisra Sharaz, Hanif Kureishi** und **Salman Rushdie** sprechen Nachkommen ehemaliger Einwanderer aus den Commonwealth Ländern zu uns über heutige Erfahrungen in ihrer Heimat, einer nunmehr „multikulturellen“ Welt. Den besonderen Reiz ihrer Texte macht aus, dass sie dabei die Schuld an der teils noch immer nicht funktionierenden Integration ethnischer Minderheiten nicht nur der mangelnden Toleranz der britischen Gesellschaft zuschreiben, sondern diese oft kritisch-aufklärerisch, oft aber auch humorvoll in eigener traditions- oder religionsspezifischer Beschränktheit sehen und diese plakatieren.

Die Auswahl der Texte entspricht der Vorgabe für das Schwerpunktthema: *One language – many voices* im Abitur 2007 in Baden-Württemberg.

Hinweise zu den Autorinnen und Autoren finden sich in Form von Kurzbiografien im Textband.

---

[1] Joseph Conrads „An Outpost of Progress“ wurde aufgenommen, obwohl es sich eigentlich um Ereignisse in der belgischen Kolonie am Kongo handelt. Die darin ironisch geäußerte Kritik am Imperialismus gilt jeder Kolonialmacht.

Die Inhalte

1. **Joseph Conrad, *An Outpost of Progress* (1898)** S. 6–26

Zwei Europäer, Kayerts als Chef und Carlier als Assistent, sollen für den Direktor einer großen Handelsgesellschaft eine heruntergekommene Station im Kongo zum Florieren bringen. Dort treffen sie als einzige andere Bewohner den Angestellten Henry Price, einen Sierra Leone-Neger, der von allen Makola genannt wird, dessen Familie und zehn weitere schwarze Arbeiter an. Der Nahrungsmittel- und Elfenbeinhandel mit den Einheimischen läuft aufgrund der trägen Arbeitsmoral der beiden Männer nur zäh. Makola organisiert jedoch überraschend eine enorme Menge besten Elfenbeins. Als sich herausstellt, dass er dafür die Entführung der zehn Arbeiter in die Sklaverei arrangiert hat, sind Kayerts und Carlier zunächst entsetzt, finden sich aber mit der Situation ab. Da nun aber die Eingeborenen aus Angst vor den vermeintlichen Sklavenhändlern die Station meiden, gehen bald die Lebensmittelvorräte zur Neige und jeglicher Handel kommt zum Erliegen. Die Beziehung der Männer spannt sich so sehr an, dass ein Streit um einige Zuckerstücke damit endet, dass Kayerts Carlier erschießt und sich anschließend selbst erhängt.
Conrads erste zur Veröffentlichung bestimmte *short story* ist eine seiner kürzesten Geschichten. Sein generelles literarisches Anliegen, größte Sparsamkeit der Erzählmittel (*narrative economy*) walten zu lassen, keine Abstriche an der Textlänge (*text length*) auf Kosten der Inhalte zu machen, und eine möglichst hohe Textdichte (*textual concentration*) zu erreichen, erfüllt er hier besonders durch den gezielten Einsatz von Symbolen, Ironie und dem auktorialen Erzähler.

---

2. **William Somerset Maugham, *The Force of Circumstance* (1928)** S. 26–48

Somerset Maughams Kurzgeschichte dreht sich um die Beziehungskrise eines britischen Kolonialbeamten in Malaysia und seiner Frau. Guy, der als Sohn britischer Eltern in Malaysia aufgewachsen ist, kommt auf Urlaub nach England, um sich zu verheiraten. In einem kleinen Hotel am Meer trifft er Doris, die mit ihrer Mutter ebenfalls Urlaub macht. Am Ende ihres vierwöchigen Aufenthalts hält Guy um die Hand der jungen Sekretärin an, die, entgegen ihres eigentlichen Vorsatzes, akzeptiert. Guy und Doris gehen gemeinsam nach Malaysia, wo Guy unerwarteter Weise an seinen alten Arbeitsplatz abkommandiert wird. Zunächst genießen die beiden ihr junges Glück und Doris ist mit ihrer neuen Situation als Ehefrau rundum zufrieden. Dann aber fällt ihr in der Nähe ihres Hauses immer wieder eine junge Malayin mit einem kleinen Kind auf. Sie wird von Bediensteten unfreundlich verjagt. Bei einem Gang durch das Dorf sieht Doris zwei Jungen, deren Hautfarbe viel heller ist als die der anderen Dorfbewohner. Schließlich bestätigt sich Doris' aufkeimender Verdacht. Guy gesteht, mit der jungen Frau über zehn Jahre hin ein Verhältnis gehabt zu haben und der Vater ihrer drei Kinder zu sein. Er begründet dieses Verhältnis mit seiner Einsamkeit an seinem neuen Arbeitsplatz, gibt Doris aber gleichzeitig zu verstehen, dass er die Frau nie geliebt habe und dass es für beide Seiten von Anfang an klar gewesen sei, dass es sich lediglich um eine zeitlich begrenzte Beziehung handeln würde. Obwohl sie ihrem Ehemann keinerlei Vorwürfe macht, verlässt sie ihn. Er gestattet daraufhin seiner ehemaligen Partnerin, zu ihm ins Haus zurückzukommen.

S. 48–54 3. **George Orwell, *Shooting an Elephant* (1936)**

Dieser 1936 in der anti-faschistischen Zeitschrift *New Writing* veröffentlichte Essay geht auf einen autobiographischen Vorfall zurück. Zehn Jahre zuvor hatte der Erzähler in seinem Dienst in Burma als *sub-divisional officer* (zweithöchster Polizeioffizier des Distrikts) in Moulmein einen Amok laufenden Elefanten erschießen müssen. Zwar hatte der Elefant einen Coolie (indischer Lastenträger aus der niedersten Kaste) getötet, aber den Erzähler quält die Tötung des Tieres dennoch. Er hatte unter dem Druck der ihn beobachtenden Menschenmenge gegen seine Überzeugung gehandelt. Er hatte Angst gehabt, von den indischen Zuschauern als schwach verspottet und verlacht zu werden.
Die Ich-Erzählung lässt sich auf abstrakter Ebene als Parabel auf den Zustand des Empires deuten, das sich selbst überlebt hat.

S. 55–74 4. **Doris Lessing, *The Second Hut* (1964)**

Doris Lessings düstere Erzählung schildert den Überlebenskampf zweier Männer unterschiedlicher Herkunft im Afrika der Kolonialzeit. Der ehemalige Offizier Major Carruthers hat seine militärische Karriere aufgegeben und führt nun in einer britischen Kolonie das Leben eines „Gentleman Farmers“. Allerdings gelingt es ihm nicht, den in ihn gesetzten Ewartungen gerecht zu werden. Seine Farm wirft nicht genug ab, um seiner Familie das Leben zu ermöglichen, das ihr aufgrund der sozialen Zugehörigkeit zusteht. Carruthers leidet weniger unter den greifbaren Auswirkungen seiner finanziellen Situation, wie beispielsweise dem primitiven Haus oder der schäbigen Einrichtung, als vielmehr unter dem moralischen Druck, dem er sich ausgesetzt sieht, weil er nicht in der Lage ist, seine Familie standesgemäß zu versorgen. Seine Frau flüchtet sich angesichts der zunehmend auswegloser werdenden Lage in eine mysteriöse Krankheit und die Kinder verbringen die meiste Zeit im Internat, dessen Finanzierung nicht mehr gesichert ist.
Die Situation eskaliert, als Carruthers den Buren Van Heerden als Farmgehilfen einstellt, denn dieser verkörpert seine schlimmsten Alpträume. Van Heerden bewegt sich aufgrund von Arbeitslosigkeit und daraus resultierendem Geldmangel auf der untersten Ebene der Gesellschaft. In Van Heerden hat Carruthers täglich vor Augen, welches Schicksal ihm drohen könnte, wenn sich sein Glück nicht wendet bzw. wenn er nicht endlich den von seiner Frau verlangten Brief nach Hause schreibt und seine Familie um Hilfe bittet.
Carruthers beschließt, für Van Heerdens Familie eine zweite Hütte bauen zu lassen. Widrige Umstände und Van Heerdens rücksichtsloses Verhalten gegenüber den Afrikanern, die auf der Farm arbeiten, verurteilen dieses Projekt von Anfang an zum Scheitern. Die neue Hütte brennt kurz nach der Fertigstellung ab und eines der Kinder Van Heerdens kommt dabei um. In Van Heerdens gleichgültiger Haltung dem Tod seines Kindes gegenüber erkennt Carruthers, dass Armut nicht nur die äußeren Umstände menschlicher Existenz, sondern auch die ihr innewohnende Humanität zerstört. Am selben Tag beschließt er, nach England zurückzukehren.

S. 75–79 5. **R. K. Narayan, *A Horse and Two Goats* (1965)**

In R. K. Narayans humorvoller Erzählung geht es im weitesten Sinne um sprachliche und kulturelle Kommunikationsprobleme. Ein amerikanischer Tourist sieht am Eingang eines indischen Dorfes eine antike Reiterstatue, die ihn so fasziniert, dass er sie erwerben und mit sich nach Amerika nehmen will. Am Straßenrand sieht er einen der Dorfbewohner, dem er sein Anliegen vorträgt. Da der Amerikaner nur Englisch, der Inder hingegen nur Tamilisch spricht, gestaltet sich die folgende Unterhaltung der beiden äußerst schwierig. Während der Amerikaner meint, mit dem Inder in Kaufverhandlungen zu treten, verteidigt sich der Inder gegen anscheinend gegen ihn erhobene Vorwürfe, ergeht sich in Lobpreisungen seines Dorfes und der Reiterstatue und gibt dem Fremden einen Überblick über die verschiedenen Inkarnationen Vishnus. Als der amerikanische Tourist dem Inder schließlich eine Banknote entgegenhält und dabei gedankenverloren dessen zwei Ziegen streichelt, wird dem Inder klar, dass der Fremde ihm etwas abkaufen will. Überglücklich wegen des unerwarteten Reichtums überlässt der Inder dem Amerikaner seine Ziegen und geht zurück zum Dorf. Währenddessen lässt sich der Amerikaner, zufrieden mit dem vermeintlichen Erwerb der Reiterstatue, zu deren Füßen nieder und wartet, bis der Alte wohl mit Männern vom Dorf kommen wird, die ihm helfen, die Statue in sein Auto zu verladen.

---

6. **Chinua Achebe, *Dead Men's Path* (1972)** S. 80–82

Chinua Achebe zeichnet mit seiner Hauptfigur Michael Obi das Bild eines jungen und ehrgeizigen Menschen, für den Modernität und Fortschritt alles bedeuten und der deshalb nicht in der Lage ist, sich in die Denkweise anderer Menschen hineinzuversetzen. Obi kommt als neuer Schulleiter an eine Schule in der Provinz. Hier sieht er die Möglichkeit, die Ziele seines Lebens – Erziehung zum Glauben an den Fortschritt und gegen überkommene Stammestraditionen – zu verwirklichen. Als er entdeckt, dass die Dorfbewohner einen zum Schulgelände gehörenden Pfad benutzen, um zu ihrem Friedhof zu kommen, verbietet er dessen Benutzung kurzerhand, ohne auf die Bitten und Einwände des Dorfpriesters einzugehen. Kurz danach stirbt eine junge Frau bei der Geburt ihres Kindes und die Dorfbewohner sehen den Grund dafür darin, dass der alte Weg, auf dem nach ihrer Überzeugung die Toten das Dorf verlassen und umgekehrt die noch nicht geborenen Kinder ins Dorf kommen, nicht mehr benutzt werden darf. Aus Rache verwüsten sie das Schulgelände. Dies geschieht just an dem Tag, an dem ein Inspektor der Schulbehörde die Schule besucht. Entsetzt über die herrschenden Zustände schreibt er einen Brief an seine Vorgesetzten und Michael Obi wird seines Amtes enthoben.

---

7. **Ngugi wa Thiong'o, *A Meeting in the* Dark (1974)** S. 83–94

Im Zentrum dieser Erzählung steht eine problematische Vater-Sohn-Beziehung, an der neben persönlichen auch religiöse und kulturelle Konflikte aufgezeigt werden. Der junge John steht kurz vor seiner Abreise nach Uganda, wo er auf ein College gehen soll. Er ist der Sohn eines eifernden Priesters, der in falsch verstandenem Pflichtgefühl seine Familie ebenso wie die Mitglieder seiner Gemeinde mit harter Hand vor der ewigen Verdammnis zu bewahren sucht. Die Unterdrückung jegliche Individualität gehört dabei ebenso zu seinen Mitteln wie offene Gewalt. Aus diesem Grund ist John nicht in der Lage, seinem Vater zu gestehen, dass ein Mädchen aus dem Dorf von ihm schwanger ist. Die junge Wamuhu hingegen erwartet von John, dass er sich zu ihr bekennt, da sie ihre Schwangerschaft nicht mehr lange verbergen kann. John kann dem Druck, der vonseiten seiner Familie und auch des Dorfes auf ihm lastet – man erwartet von ihm, dass er das Dorf verlässt und in einem fremden Land seine Bildung vollendet – schließlich nichts mehr entgegensetzen. Bei seinem letzten Treffen mit Wamuhu versucht er, sich der Verantwortung ihr gegenüber mit Geld zu entziehen. Als Wamuhu sich weigert, das Geld anzunehmen, erwürgt er sie.

---

8. **Muriel Spark, *The Black Madonna* (1963)** S. 95–111

Das Leben eines Ehepaares in der englischen Provinz wird von der Statue einer schwarzen Madonna nachhaltig beeinflusst. Lou und Raymond sind seit einiger Zeit verheiratet und haben sich inzwischen damit abgefunden, dass sie keine Kinder haben. Als Raymond sich zweier Gastarbeiter aus der Karibik annimmt, gerät das wohlgeordnete Leben des Ehepaares in Bewegung. Besonders der zurückhaltende Henry gewinnt die Herzen von Lou und Raymond und wird fast so etwas wie ein Familienmitglied. Als er andeutet, dass er kein gläubiger Mensch ist, bittet Lou die schwarze Madonna, eine erst kürzlich in ihrer Kirche aufgestellte Statue, um Henrys Rückkehr zum Glauben und ihr Gebet wird erhört. Da der schwarzen Madonna auch von anderer Seite wundertätige Kräfte zugesprochen werden, entschließt sich Lou dazu, die Madonna um ein Kind zu bitten. Lou wird schwanger. Groß ist jedoch das Entsetzen beider Eltern, als Lou ein schwarzes Kind zur Welt bringt. Raymond verdächtigt zunächst einen der beiden Gastarbeiter, aber Bluttests beweisen eindeutig, dass es sich bei dem Kind um Lous und Raymonds Tochter handelt. Schließlich stellt sich heraus, dass es in Lous Familie vor einigen Generationen wohl tatsächlich einen Farbigen gegeben hat und dass die dunkle Hautfarbe zu Lous Erbgut gehört. Unfähig das eigene Kind anzunehmen, beschließen Lou und Raymond ihre Tochter zur Adoption freizugeben.

S. 111–126

9. **Quaisra Shahraz, *A Pair of Jeans* (1988/2004)**
Miriam ist eine junge Frau, die zwischen zwei Kulturen steht. Außerhalb ihres Elternhauses ist sie eine in ein westliches Wertesystem eingebundene Studentin, in ihrer Familie ist sie jedoch eine östlichen Traditionen verbundene gehorsame Tochter. Wie sehr Miriam unter dieser Doppelrolle leidet, wird ihr selbst und damit dem Leser bewusst, als sie eines Tages von ihren zukünftigen Schwiegereltern in ihrer westlichen Kleidung, Jeans, einem bauchfreien Oberteil und einer engen Lederjacke, gesehen wird. Obwohl Miriam sofort ihre Kleider wechselt und sich damit in das Inbild einer gehorsamen Tochter bzw. Schwiegertochter verwandelt, brechen die Eltern ihres Verlobten das Gespräch über die anstehende Hochzeit ab und lösen am folgenden Tag die Verlobung. Die Autorin bietet zwei Schlussversionen an. In dem neuen Schlussteil begegnet dem Leser eine sehr viel selbstbewusstere und unabhängigere Miriam. Sie setzt sich mit ihrem Verlobten Farook in Verbindung, um die Situation selbst zu klären.

S. 126–135

10. **Hanif Kureishi, *My Son the Fanatic* (1994)**
Hanif Kureishi beschreibt in *My Son the Fanatic* die Situation eines Vaters, der machtlos miterleben muss, wie sich sein Sohn einer Gruppe religiöser Fanatiker zuwendet. Parvez, ein pakistanischer Einwanderer in Großbritannien, verdient sein Geld als Taxifahrer. Sein ganzer Stolz ist sein Sohn Ali, dem er eine gute Ausbildung und damit, wie er meint, ein besseres Leben ermöglichen will. Ali jedoch scheint plötzlich nichts mehr an den Dingen zu liegen, die ihm früher wichtig waren. Parvez vermutet zunächst, sein Sohn sei drogenabhängig. Schließlich wird ihm jedoch klar, dass Ali sich von allen weltlichen Dingen getrennt hat, weil er sich in seinem Leben auf seiner Meinung nach wirklich Wichtiges konzentrieren möchte. Ali wird zum religiösen Eiferer, der alles Westliche als nicht gottgefällig verdammt. Er macht seinem Vater bittere Vorwürfe und verurteilt dessen gotteslästerliches Leben, das sich an westlichem Konsum und Vergnügen orientiert. Parvez bemüht sich, seinen Sohn zu verstehen und auf ihn zuzugehen, stößt jedoch auf Ablehnung. Schließlich kommt es zum Bruch als Parvez auf seinen betenden Sohn einschlägt, wohl wissend, dass er ihn weder durch Verständnis noch durch Gewalt zu sich zurückholen kann.

S. 135–141

11. **Salman Rushdie, *Good Advice is Rarer than Rubies* (1994)**
Die junge und attraktive Miss Rehana begibt sich zum britischen Konsulat in einer größeren Stadt, um ein Einreisevisum nach Großbritannien zu erhalten. Dort lebt der

Mann, den ihr ihre inzwischen verstorbenen Eltern als Ehemann ausgewählt haben, den sie selbst aber nie gesehen hat. Vor den Toren des Konsulats trifft Rehana Muhammad Ali, einen nicht ganz seriösen Geschäftsmann, der den so genannten „Tuesday women", Frauen, die jeden Dienstag zum Konsulat kommen, um Einreisevisa nach Großbritannien zu beantragen, mit Rat und Tat zur Seite steht. Auch Rehana versucht er seine Ratschläge im Umgang mit den Behörden zu verkaufen. Als Rehana jedoch merkt, dass Ali mit nicht ganz legalen Mitteln arbeitet, wendet sie sich von ihm ab, ohne einen seiner Ratschläge zu befolgen. Mit Bangen erwartet der von Rehanas Anmut und Schönheit faszinierte Ali ihre Rückkehr. Als Rehana nach einiger Zeit aus dem Tor des britischen Konsulats tritt, erfährt Ali, dass seine Befürchtungen eingetreten sind. Die junge Frau hat keine Einreisegenehmigung nach Großbritannien erhalten. Zu seinem Erstaunen aber ist sie alles andere als unglücklich. Muhammad Ali wird klar, dass Rehana Indien nie wirklich verlassen wollte, weil sie dort glücklich ist.

Story	**Setting**	**Protagonists**	**Plot**
An Outpost of Progress pp. 6–26	Africa/ [Belgian] Congo	Two white men, Kayerts and Carlier; Makola, an African	Two white men do not survive their job at a remote trading station in Africa.
The Force of Circumstance pp. 26–48	Malaya	Doris and Guy, a British couple; Guy's former Malay lover	The marriage of Doris and Guy breaks up because Guy's former lover asserts her rights.
Shooting an Elephant pp. 48–54	(former) Burma/ Moulmein	British subdivisional-officer	First person narration reflecting on the shooting of an elephant which ran amok.
The Second Hut pp. 55–74	Africa	Major Carruthers; Van Heerden; their wives; natives	Carruthers gives up his dream of a farm in Africa when he realises due to Van Heerden's example how failure can destroy human existence.
A Horse and Two Goats pp. 75–79	India	an American tourist; an Indian farmer	The American and the Indian cannot understand each other so instead of buying an ancient statue, the American ends up with two goats.
Dead Men's Path pp. 80–82	Africa	Michael Obi, a headmaster; Obi's wife; an old priest	In trying to make his dream of a modern school come true, Obi neglects the needs of others and brings about his own failure.

A Meeting in the Dark pp. 83–94	Africa	John, the son of a preacher; his father; Wamuhu, John's girlfriend	John cannot come to terms with the pressure his family and friends exert on him and so kills his girlfriend, who is pregnant by him.
The Black Madonna pp. 95–111	the North of England	Lou and Raymond, a married couple; Henry and Oxford, two Jamaican immigrants	Lou and Raymond are pious Catholics. Lou prays to the Black Madonna for a baby but later cannot accept the child because it is black.
A Pair of Jeans pp. 111–126	the North of England	Miriam, daughter of Indian immigrants; her parents; her prospective parents-in-law; her fiancé	Miriam is torn between two cultures, as symbolised by the way she dresses. The alternative ending of the story shows a more self-confident Miriam than the first one.
My Son the Fanatic pp. 126–135	England	Parvez, a Punjabi taxi-driver; Ali, his son; Bettina, a prostitute	Parvez cannot prevent his son from joining a group of religious fanatics.
Good Advice is Rarer than Rubies pp. 135–141	India	Miss Rehana; Muhammad Ali	Miss Rehana tries to get a visa for Great Britain. She meets Muhammad Ali who offers to help her. She does not take his advice, is denied a visa and explains to Ali why she is happy nevertheless.

Vorbemerkungen zur Konzeption des Unterrichtsmodells, zum Einsatz der Audio-CD und der Autorenbiografien im Textband

Die ***Components*** ergeben sich aus der Chronologie und den thematischen Schwerpunkten der Geschichten. Dennoch ist die Reihenfolge flexibel handhabbar. Genauso kann jede Geschichte unabhängig und eigenständig unterrichtet werden.
Der Umfang der *short stories* ist sehr verschieden, daher wird ein Hinweis gegeben, wenn eine vorbereitende Lektüre der Schülerinnen und Schüler erwartet wird. Ansonsten wird der Text im Unterrichtsverlauf erarbeitet.
In allen *Components* wird weitgehend textimmanent verfahren, d. h., dass es hauptsächlich um die Charakterisierung der Protagonisten und die Analyse der Beziehungen zueinander geht. Dies und die Erschließung des jeweiligen *plots* geschieht auf vielfältige Weise im Sinne eines handlungsorientierten Unterrichts, in dem die Förderung der Sprachkompetenz der Lerngruppe im Vordergrund steht. Wir empfehlen die hier verfolgte induktive Verfahrensweise mit der schülerzentriert Merkmale und Kernaussagen im traditionellen Unterrichtsgespräch, in wechselnden Sozialformen (Partner- und Gruppenarbeit, *fish bowl, hot seat* etc.) und kreativ (*role plays, diary entries, letters*) erarbeitet werden. Unterstützt wird dies durch von der Lerngruppe zu bearbeitende ***Worksheets*** und ***Task sheets***, wenn es um die Durchführung von anspruchsvollen, meist allerdings auch zeitaufwändigen Aktivitäten geht. Die ***Info sheets*** und ***Solution sheets*** bieten zum einen zusätzliches Material und Musterlösungen, ermöglichen aber andererseits auch eine effektive Verkürzung des Vorgehens. Dazu können sie alternativ zu einer zeitintensiven Phase als eigene Texte von der Lerngruppe versprachlicht bzw. auf ihre Aussagen hin analysiert werden. Die **Unterkapitel der *Components*** entsprechen je ungefähr einer Unterrichtsstunde. Sie sind in Einstiegsphasen, Erarbeitungs-, Sicherungs-, und Vertiefungsphasen eingeteilt. Es wird jeweils eine Hausaufgabe vorgeschlagen, die gegebenenfalls stundenvorbereitend sein kann.
Der **Einsatz der Audio-CD** ist gekennzeichnet. Die Unterrichtsentwürfe beziehen diese entsprechend ein. Besonders reizvoll ist die Vertonung von Chinua Achebe's *Dead Men's Path.* Hier wurde ein afrikanischer Sprecher für die Aufnahme gewonnen. Sein stark akzentuiertes Sprechen kann im Sinne des Themas „One Language – Many Voices“ über den Inhalt der Geschichte hinaus als eine „Echo“-Wirkung gedeutet werden: so oder so ähnlich klingt das Englisch dort, wo es koloniale Amtssprache wurde.
Zu jeder Geschichte werden **Themen für Referate** beziehungsweise für die gleichwertig festgestellten Schülerleistungen (gfS), wie sie in Baden-Württemberg abiturrelevant gefordert werden, vorgeschlagen. Sie sind sehr allgemein gehalten, da die Lehrerin oder der Lehrer die Spezifizierung des Themas vom einzelnen Schüler oder der Schülerin abhängig machen wird. Anhand der im **Textband** beigefügten Materialien zum historischen Hintergrund ergibt sich ein Ansatz zur landeskundlichen Erweiterung der Einheit, die je nach Bedarf durch aktuelle Schulbücher oder andere Medien ausgeweitet werden kann.
Wenn die gemeinsame Lektüre der **Autorenporträts** in der Textausgabe als zu eintönig empfunden wird, können diese von Schülerinnen und Schülern als Kurzvortrag präsentiert werden. Mit den annotierten Lebensläufen wird zusätzlich

kulturelles Wissen über die Auswirkungen des Kolonialismus transportiert. Das Wiedererkennen biografischer Elemente in den Texten, wie die Problematik der Akkulturation (*clash of cultures*) oder der *gender role* in der anderen Kultur oder Tradition, dürfte für die Schüler und Schülerinnen eine zusätzliche Motivation sein, sich mit diesen zu beschäftigen.

Referatthemen und Themen für gleichwertig festgestellte Schülerleistungen (gfS)

Joseph Conrad, *An Outpost of Progress* (1898)

- *Heart of Darkness* – a novella by Joseph Conrad
- *Apocalypse Now* – the film version of *Heart of Darkness*
- Slave and ivory trade in Africa (siehe auch D. Lessing)

W. Somerset Maugham, *The Force of Circumstance* (1928)

- British colonialism in South-East Asia
- British life in the Asian colonies

George Orwell, *Shooting an Elephant* (1936)

- Burma/Myanmar
- George Orwell, *Burmese Days*

Doris Lessing, *The Second Hut* (1964)

- Colonial powers in Africa
- Colonial life in Africa
- The Boer War

R. K. Narayan: *A Horse and Two Goats* (1965)

- Hinduism
- India – the jewel in the crown

Chinua Achebe, *Dead Men's Path* (1972)

- Tradition and progress
- [Varieties of English in Africa/ English as official language in the colonies]

Ngugi wa Thiong'o, *A Meeting in the Dark* (1974)

- Female circumcision: Women in Islamic countries
- The Christian mission in Africa

Muriel Spark, *The Black Madonna* (1963)

- Christian saints and miracles
- Genetics
- Jamaican immigration to Great Britain

Qaisra Shahraz, *A Pair of Jeans* (1988/2004)

- Women in Islamic societies
- The emancipation of women
- The tradition of tolerance
- Brick Lane – a novel by Monica Ali

Hanif Kureishi, *My Son the Fanatic* (1994)

- A comparison with the film
- Religious fanaticism
- The Salman Rushdie outrage
- Immigration from Pakistan and the Pakistan-India conflict

Salman Rushdie, *Good Advice is Rarer than Rubies* (1994)

- The *fatwah* against Salman Rushdie (in Verbindung mit Biografie)
- Indian immigration to the UK
- The emancipation of women in Asia (siehe auch Q. Sharaz)

W. Somerset Maugham, *The Yellow Streak* (Excerpt)

streak a long thin mark or line of a different substance or colour from its surroundings

The two prahus were dropping easily down-stream, one a few yards ahead of the other, and in the first sat the two white men. After seven weeks on the rivers they were glad to know that they would lodge that night in a civilised house. To Izzart, who had been in Borneo since the war, the Dyak houses and their feasts were of course an old story; but Campion, though new to the country and at first amused by the strangeness, hankered too now for chairs to sit on and a bed to sleep in. The Dyaks were hospitable, but no one could say that there was much comfort to be found in their houses, and there was a monotony in the entertainment they offered a guest which presently grew somewhat wearisome. [...] Campion looked at the shabby silver watch on his wrist. It could not be long now before they reached their destination.

"What sort of chap is Hutchinson?" he asked. "I don't know him. I believe he's a very good sort."

Hutchinson was the Resident in whose house they were to spend the night, and they had sent on a Dyak in a canoe to announce their arrival.

"Well, I hope he's got some whisky. I've drunk enough arak to last me a lifetime."

Campion was a mining engineer whom the Sultan on his way to England had met at Singapore, and finding him at a loose end had commissioned to go to Sembulu and see whether he could discover any mineral which might be profitably worked. He sent Willis, the Resident at Kuala Solor, instructions to afford him every facility, and Willis had put him in the care of Izzart because Izzart spoke both Malay and Dyak like a native. This was the third trip they had made into the interior, and now Campion was to go home with his reports. They were to catch the *Sultan Ahmed,* which was due to pass the mouth of the river at dawn on the next day but one, and with any luck should reach Kuala Solor on the same afternoon. They were both glad to get back to it. There was tennis and golf there, and the comforts of civilisation. Izzart was glad, too, that he would have other society than Campion's. He gave him a side-long glance. He was a little man with a big, bald head, and though certainly fifty, strong and wiry; he had quick, shining blue eyes and a stubbly, grey moustache. He was seldom without an old briar pipe between his broken and discoloured teeth. He was neither clean nor neat, his khaki shorts were ragged and his singlet torn; he was wearing now a battered topee. He had knocked about the world since he was eighteen and had been in South Africa, in China and in Mexico. He was good company; he could tell a story well, and he was prepared to drink and drink again with anyone he met. They had got on very well together, but Izzart had never felt quite at home with him.

prahu boats

the war *here:* World War I (1914–1918)

to hanker to have a strong desire to do sth

Dyak native people of Borneo and their language

wearisome boring

Resident a person living steadily at one place

arak alcohol distilled from grain, rice, sugar cane, etc

at a loose end without any occupation

Sultan Ahmed name of a ship

bald *glatzköpfig*

wiry lean, thin

briar pipe *Bruyèrepfeife*

ragged torn

singlet *ärmelloses Unterhemd*

battered topee *zerbeulter Tropenhelm*

Though they joked and laughed together, got drunk together, Izzart felt that there was no intimacy between them: for all the cordiality of their relations they remained nothing but acquaintances. He was very sensitive to the impression he made on others, and behind Campion's joviality he had felt a certain coolness; those shining blue eyes had summed him up; and it vaguely irritated Izzart that Campion had formed an opinion of him, and he did not quite know what it was. He was exasperated by the possibility that this common little man did not think entirely well of him. He desired to be liked and admired. He wanted to be popular. […] Izzart and Hutchinson grew a little drunk. Presently Hutchinson told Izzart that he lived with a Malay girl, and had a couple of children by her. […] "I shall never do it myself," said Izzart. "After all, one may want to get married and then it means all sorts of botherations." "But who wants to get married? What a life for a white woman. I wouldn't ask a white woman to live here for anything in the world."

"Of course it's a matter of taste. If I have any kiddies I'm going to see that they have a white mother."
Hutchinson looked down at the little dark-skinned child he held in his arms. He gave a faint smile.

"It's funny how you get to like them," he said. "When they're your own it doesn't seem to matter that they've got a touch of the tarbrush."

The woman gave the child a look, and getting up said she would take it back to bed. "I should think we'd better all turn in," said Hutchinson. "God knows what the time is."

Izzart went to his room and threw open the shutters which his boy Hassan, whom he was travelling with had closed. […] "They've got no right to have them," he said to himself. "They've got no chance in the world. Ever." (848 words)

W. Somerset Maugham: *The Yellow Streak.* In: Collected Short Stories Vol. One. New York: Penguin 1992

acquaintance not a close friendship

joviality cheerfulness, friendliness

botheration trouble

tar *Teer*

Assignments

1. Compare the two men Izzart and Campion. Why does Izzart not completely feel at ease with Campion?
2. Izzart's good humour is gone after Hutchinson's presentation of his half-caste child and Malay woman. Explain his reaction and his inner conviction: "They've got no right to have them. […] They've got no chance in the world. Ever." (ll. 77–78)

Choose one of the following two creative tasks:

Creative task 1:

The next morning Izzart and Campion leave for Kuala Solor. They get caught in a Bore (heavy sea-storm) and they nearly drown. Izzart hears Campion cry for help but is too exhausted and too afraid to help him. Izzart reaches the shore. Instead of sending help, he declares Campion dead. Meanwhile, some Malays in dug-outs have rescued Campion. Izzart's first thought is: "I wish to God he'd been drowned. Then I'd have been safe." Why is Izzart so terribly afraid of Campion after the incident? Write down his diary entry drawing conclusions from the information given in the text.

Creative task 2:

Hutchinson, though he did not show it to Izzart at the moment of their conversation, feels offended and threatened by Izzart's arrogant behaviour and reaction towards his Malay woman and child. He has suspicions about a possible "yellow streak" in Izzart's blood and remembers having heard a rumour about Izzart's mother in London. He wants to find out the truth and therefore writes a letter to a mutual friend in London.
Write that letter, expressing Hutchinson's fear that Izzart might cause him problems on his return home to London.

Erwartungshorizont zu Klausur 1

Zu 1: Izzart and Campion are working for the Sultan of Sembulu in Borneo after World War I. They have both had many experiences with other cultures. Izzart has lived in Borneo for seven years; Campion has been to South Africa, China and Mexico to work as an engineer. Although they can cope with the natives, they have a strong desire for "civilized comforts" of European standard, even if these might be as simple as sitting on some chairs and sleeping in a bed after a long journey through the jungles of Borneo. After their third trip together, this is meant to be their final journey back to Kuala Solor, where they will find the pleasures and luxury they long for: tennis and golf and good conversation. Izzart, in particular, is hoping for other company than Campion's.
Campion is an ugly fellow with no sense of decent outer appearance as he wears a shabby silver watch, and dirty and torn clothes. Although his broken and discoloured teeth are disgusting, he is well liked by others. He is a very sociable and talkative man and can make friends by drinking large quantities with anyone who is prepared to let him join in.
Izzart is quite different from him. Described as "very sensitive to the impression he made on others" (ll. 51–52), he is an officer with a slightly arrogant attitude towards the others and, most obviously, towards the natives. In contrast to Campion, he is not an outgoing type and keeps a cautious distance to the others. His behaviour contradicts his utmost wish to be popular and well-liked by other people.
Izzart does not really take a liking to Campion because of his appearance and behaviour. His shabbiness, drinking attitude and generous friendliness towards other people remind Izzart of all the bad qualities that are associated with natives. He is also jealous of Campion. Campion, although by no means as handsome or sophisticated as he is, seems to have it all. Izzart badly wants to be popular and to be admired, but he does not have the easy-going ways of Campion that make it possible to befriend others or impress them.

Zu 2: Izzart's cold and unfriendly attitude towards Hutchinson's half-caste children must be based on his observations of half-castes or experiences with them. He knows about the prejudices against half-castes and that white people pretend to be their friends but laugh at them as soon as they turn their backs. He seems to have some respect for the Malay women, although he thinks a marriage-like relationship and even having children with one of them might cause problems getting a "proper" wife back home in England. So he rejects Hutchinson's way of life.

Creative task 1 – Diary entry

The trip down to Kuala Solor was not the pleasant cruise I had expected it to be. Looking forward to all the fine civilized amusements waiting there after three trips with Campion, that brute, we had taken the warnings of the Bore too lightly and when we left Hutchinson's house, we headed straight into disaster. But it is not surviving that terrible storm and the fight against those walls of waves that make my blood freeze – it is much worse – today, out there on the angry river, I made a fatal mistake. I lacked courage and was not able to suppress or overcome a feeling of malicious joy that could have caused Campion's death. Both are manifestations of the influence of this evil native blood in me and now I am sure that it can only be a question of time before my well-kept secret is revealed. I will be dismissed from all honours and left without any chances in London. I am done for. It is pure irony that of all creatures, it has to be that vulgar and ugly little gnome Campion who now will be master of my fate. I wish to God he had been drowned. Then I would have been safe. It was a real shock when the

Malay boys brought him up to the shore. Hassan and I really thought he must have died in the gigantic waves caused by the Bore that broke over our boat and capsized it. I am sure Hassan did not hear him cry for help. But I am not sure that he did not recognize that I swam away from him. I was struggling for life myself but I could have sent Hassan back to help him after I had solid ground under my feet. Did I give up too easily or did I deliberately leave him behind to get rid of that bloody fool? Why did he grin so devilishly when he asked me if I had not heard him shout? Did he recognize that I was lying when I said I had neither heard nor seen him anymore? He will tell this story like all his other stories of those half-caste cowards and make a laughing stock of me. It won't take him long to find out about mother after he has returned to London. Then I am really done for. He will report me to my superiors and reveal that I am a pretender, a dirty Eurasian who failed in his duty: to care for him – that shabby guy – and to save him from danger. He will ruin me in no time. I cannot let him reveal my secret. That must not bet allowed to happen …

Creative task 2 – Letter by Hutchinson

Dear George,
I know it has been a long time since I have written to you. But today there is a really good reason to let you know that all of us – Molly, the kids and me – are still alive and well out here. The world is sometimes a truly small place – imagine – today I met a friend of yours, a rather dark and – I must say – somewhat stiff guy called Izzart. He accompanied an engineer who also works for the Sultan to several places that might be profitable for mining. Anyway, it is Izzart that I want to talk to you about.
Our conversation started quite well. We talked among other things about our schooldays and soon discovered that we had gone to the same school in London and so had some friends in common. We soon forgot about the engineer who could not join in the conversation for he had never gone to any public school, you see. He left early and so Izzart and I had some more drinks. We had almost finished our jolly talk when – I don't know what had come over me – I told him that I had a Malay woman and kids from her. His reaction was more than irritating. As a matter of fact, I am still angry about his arrogant and offending tone, as he told me he would never take a native woman but only marry a white one to have white children with her! I agreed with him pointing out that it was the usual custom of us men out here in the wilderness to have someone to keep the house and of course to then get married to a good white woman at home. But when he left for bed, I suddenly became furious, I mean, when I look at little Pete and his sisters – they are so cute, they are my children and I will provide for them and Molly.
Nevertheless, he emphasized troubles one could get into at home. It seems to me that the guy appears to be friendly only on the surface and could turn out to be rather malicious. Actually, I remembered having heard unpleasant things about him – it must be ages ago. He was not very popular at school because when he came to England he didn't speak much English. Wasn't he raised by an aunt and brought from Borneo speaking only Malay? There was also some rumour about his mother. Could you find out more, and soon? You see, up till now you have been the only person who knows about Molly and the kids and you promised to keep that knowledge private. He may be right, and on my return to London next year, my chances with that pretty Windsor lady might crumble to pieces if she found out, you know.
Please try to collect useful information so that I can keep Izzart in check, one never knows ...

Kind regards,
Yours Pete

The New Empire within Britain
by Salman Rushdie

Britain isn't South Africa. I am reliably informed of this. Nor is it Nazi Germany. I've got that on the best authority as well. You may feel that these two statements are not exactly the most dramatic of revelations. But it's remarkable how often they, or similar statements, are used to counter the arguments of anti-racist campaigners. 'Things aren't as bad as all that', we are told, 'you exaggerate, you're indulging in special pleading, you must be paranoid.' So let me concede at once that, as far as I know, there are no pass laws here. Inter-racial marriages are permitted. And Auschwitz hasn't been rebuilt in the Home Counties. I find it odd, however, that those who use such absences as defences rarely perceive that their own statements indicate how serious things have become. Because if the defence for Britain is that mass extermination of racially impure persons hasn't yet begun, or that the principle of white supremacy hasn't actually been enshrined in the constitution, then something must have gone very wrong indeed. I want to suggest that racism is not a side-issue, in contemporary Britain; that it's not a peripheral minority affair. I believe that Britain is undergoing a critical phase of its post-colonial period, and this crisis is not simply economic or political. It's a crisis of the whole culture, of the society's entire sense of itself. And racism is only the most clearly visible part of this crisis, the tip of the kind of iceberg that sinks ships.

Now I don't suppose many of you think of the British Empire as a subject worth losing much sleep over. After all, surely the one thing one can confidently say about that roseate age of England's precedence, when the map of half the world blushed with pleasure as it squirmed beneath the Pax Britannica, is that it's over, isn't it? Give or take a Falkland Island, the imperial sun has set. […] But the connection I want to make is this: that those same attitudes are in operation right here as well, here in what E. P. Thompson has described as the last colony of the British Empire. It sometimes seems that the British authorities, no longer capable of exporting governments, have chosen instead to import a new Empire, a new community of subject peoples of whom they think, and with whom they can deal, in very much the same way as their predecessors thought of and dealt with 'the fluttered folk and wild', the 'new-caught, sullen peoples, half-devil and half-child', who made up, for Rudyard Kipling, the White Man's Burden. In short, if we want to understand British racism – and without understanding no improvement is possible – it's impossible even to begin to grasp the nature of the beast unless we accept its historical roots. Four hundred years of conquest and looting, four centuries of being told that

reliable that can be trusted

revelation a fact that people are made aware of
to counter *kontern*

to indulge in *schwelgen*

to concede to admit that sth is true, logical etc

Home Counties counties around London

to perceive to notice or become aware of sth

to enshrine to make a law, right etc official

peripheral marginal

roseate pink in colour (referring to the skin of the British colonizers as seen by the natives)
to blush to become red in the face
to squirm *nervös hin und her rutschen*
Falkland Islands a group of over 100 islands in the S Atlantic; a British crown colony; invaded by Argentina, who had long laid claim to the islands, on 2 April 1982; recaptured by a British expeditionary force on 14 June 1982
sullen silent and bad-tempered
White Man's Burden the supposed duty of the White Race to bring education and Western culture to the non-white inhabitants of their colonies
the nature of the beast *here:* the real reasons behind racism
looting *Plünderung*

you are superior to the Fuzzy-Wuzzies and the wogs, leave their stain. This stain has seeped into every part of the culture, the language and daily life; and nothing much has been done to wash it out.

For proof of the existence of this stain, we can look, for instance, at the huge, undiminished appetite of white Britons for television series, films, plays and books all filled with nostalgia for the Great Pink Age. Or think about the ease with which the English language allows the terms of racial abuse to be coined: wog, frog, kraut, dago, spic, yid, coon, nigger, Argie. Can there be another language with so wide-ranging a vocabulary of racist denigration? […] One of the key concepts of imperialism was that military superiority implied cultural superiority, and this enabled the British to condescend to and repress cultures far older than their own; and it still does. For the citizens of the new, imported Empire, for the colonized Asians and blacks of Britain, the police force represents that colonizing army, those regiments of occupation and control.

Now the peoples whom I've characterized, as members of a new colony would probably be described by most of you as 'immigrants'. […] (680 words)

from Salman Rushdie: Imaginary Homelands. Essays and Criticism 1981–1991, London: Granta Books, 1991, pp. 129–132

Fuzzy-Wuzzy, wog derogative terms for indigenous people
stain dirty mark

to coin *prägen*

wog, frog ... derogative names for different groups of foreigners
denigration unfair criticism

to condescend to to treat people in an insulting way because you think they are below your social or professional position

Assignments

1. Does Rushdie agree with the general public opinion that those who are afraid of racism are simply paranoid and the Empire is over and done with?
2. What is the reason for growing racism in Britain according to the text?
3. What does the "new Empire" consist of?
4. How does Rushdie try to grab the reader's attention for his claims?

*5. Writers like Ngugi wa Thiong'o refuse to write in English any longer. What does Rushdie say about the English language? Should he also start writing in his native language? Use your information about the author's biography.

*6. Could Rushdie's attitude towards Britain, as expressed in the text above, be detected in the short story *Good Advice is Rarer than Rubies* as well?

Erwartungshorizont zu Klausur 2:

Zu 1: No, he does not. Rushdie warns against the belittlement of racist attitudes as expressed by those who defend their tolerance by pointing out that foreigners are not treated like the Jews in the Third Reich or as bad as the blacks in South Africa suffering under the apartheid system. He reveals the great danger that lies behind this proclaimed tolerance. Rushdie mentions a very recent case of imperialist action, when Britain took over the Falkland Islands in a battle to secure their military interests there. He also feels that the interest that Britons show in films romanticizing the age of colonization is another symptom for their clinging to their imperial past.

Zu 2: Britain is suffering from a crisis that is not restricted to economic or political problems. It is deeply involved in a cultural crisis caused by the clash of old, traditional but obsolete, governmental and social structures and the needs and rightful demands of people who have emancipated themselves from their imposed inferiority.

Zu 3: The new Empire is made up of all the immigrants that have been "invited" to Great Britain. In Great Britain, the people coming from the colonies are treated as disgracefully as their forefathers in the days of the colonizers in the colonies abroad. The Britons still feel superior to the immigrants. Many of them still believe in the concept of racial supremacy that has been propagated for over four hundred years and that fosters their racist ideas. The new means of control and pressure is now the police whereas it used to be the colonizing army.

Zu 4: Rushdie's text is very ironic and provocative. The proposal that the condition for the immigrants could be worse than the treatment of the Jews during the Third Reich, for example, is very extreme. The discussion is thus triggered off. He uses poignant metaphors like "the tip of the kind of iceberg that sinks ships" to emphasize the impact of racism. Sarcastically, he draws the reader's attention to the fact that there is still imperialist energy in the system: "After all, surely the one thing one can confidently say about that roseate age of England's precedence, when the map of half the world blushed with pleasure as it squirmed beneath the Pax Britannica, is that it's over, isn't it? Give or take a Falkland Island, the imperial sun has set."

*5 und *6 gehen über den Text hinaus und setzen zusätzliche Kenntnisse voraus:

Zu 5: Die Schülerinnen und Schüler sollten zunächst die Informationen aus dem Text („Or think about the ease with which the English language allows the terms of racial abuse to be coined: wog, frog, kraut, dago, spic, yid, coon, nigger, Argie. Can there be another language with so wide-ranging a vocabulary of racist denigration?") in eigene Worte fassen und dann die Frage in Verbindung mit Rushdies Biografie und *fatwah*-Bedrohung erörtern.

Zu 6: Wenn die *short story Good Advice is Rarer than Rubies* behandelt wurde, bietet sich die Frage an, obgleich die Geschichte in keinem direkten Zusammenhang mit Rushdies Text steht. Die Antwort kann durch eine enge Wortbegrenzung beschränkt werden, um nicht allzu künstliche Bezüge zu erhalten.

Rushdie's attitude towards Britain here is that he still sees imperialism and racism at work. Given the bad treatment of the immigrants and their new role as second class subjects, Britain is certainly no place to be longed for.

Miss Rehana is not so keen on going to Great Britain and joining her fiancé. The other women are different and want to emigrate as soon as possible to seek their fortune there. Rehana wants to stay in her culture where she has her place and individual freedom. In Britain, she would be a kind of slave to her husband and would always be an outsider to society.

Notizen:

Component 1: Colonial Encounters

Getting started

Zur Einführung in die Unterrichtseinheit dienen die Seiten *Getting started* des Textbandes (S. 4 und 5). Die Schülerinnen und Schüler können anhand der Aufgabenstellung auf die Inhalte der *short stories* eingestimmt werden:

> This collage depicts scenes, symbols and characters from some of the short stories you are going to read.
>
> 1. What will they be about? Guess first without browsing the book.
>
> Auch die andere Aufgabe:
>
> 2. Associate your ideas with the name of the collection "Echoes of the Empire" and the individual titles of the stories.

stellt eine Verbindung zum Leitthema der Schwerpunkteinheit *One Language – Many Voices* her. Hier können die Schülerinnen und Schüler ihr Hintergrundwissen über den Kolonialismus aktivieren. Dabei können sie sich über das Vermächtnis der ehemaligen Kolonialmacht, die englische Sprache als „legacy of the Empire" anhand der Bilder austauschen. So zeigt die rechte Bildseite Szenen aus den Geschichten, die in den Kolonien spielen: Elefant – *Shooting an Elephant;* Afrikanische Mutter mit Baby im Huckepack vor Strohhütte – *The Second Hut;* Dampfer – *An Outpost of Progress* und *The Force of Circumstance;* die Ziegen – *A Horse and Two Goats.* Der Hintergrund deutet einen Urwald an. Als Kontrast dazu ist die linke Seite mit einer europäischen Großstadt hinterlegt. Die Geschichten der *Components Cross-Cultural Experiences* und *Postcolonial Consequences* zeigen einerseits den Einfluss der europäischen Kultur auf die Menschen in den Kolonien, andererseits wird die multikulturelle Lebenswelt aus der Perspektive der Einwanderer dargestellt. Die Bilder deuten auf mögliche Konflikte hin, die beim Zusammentreffen verschiedener Religionen und Traditionen auftreten können (schwarze Madonna – *The Black Madonna;* drei mohammedanische junge Frauen und drei modern gekleidete multiethnische junge Frauen – *A Pair of Jeans;* betender junger Mohammedaner – *My Son the Fanatic).* Der britische Pass soll den Lebensraum Großbritannien verdeutlichen, hat aber auch Bezug zur Geschichte *Good Advice is Rarer than Rubies,* in der eine junge Inderin bewusst auf die Möglichkeit, nach England emigrieren zu können, verzichtet.
Die Collage könnte provokativ eingesetzt werden. Im Sinne von Kiplings Idee der „White Man's Burden" und darwinistisch begründeter Kultivierung der „Wilden" bietet sie vielfache Ansatzpunkte. Ein möglicher Impuls wäre:

> Isn't it good for those people in the pictures on the right side of the collage to be in Britain? They can enjoy the British culture and do not need to live in the jungle or in an undeveloped country anymore. What is your opinion?

Hier wird es davon abhängen, ob die historischen Hintergründe zum Kolonialismus und dem heutigen multikulturellen Großbritannien bekannt sind oder ob sich nun eine solche Einführung anschließen soll. Für beides eignen sich die Hintergrundinformationen im Anhang des Textbandes. Die erste Kurzgeschichte *An Outpost of Progress* schließt sich als Illustration der Zustände in den Kolonien an, als das Empire den imperialistischen Zenit durchwanderte.

Joseph Conrad, *An Outpost of Progress* (1898)

1.1 Building up expectations

Als *pre-reading activity* sollen durch eine Mind-Map Erwartungen an die Geschichte geäußert werden. Auf diese wird später wieder zurückgegriffen, wenn es unter anderem um die Entlarvung als ironische literarische Darstellung des Kolonialismus geht.

Joseph Conrad's short story is called *An Outpost of Progress.* What do you think an outpost will be?
What do we understand by "progress"?

Die Schülerbeiträge werden als Mind-Map an der Tafel gesammelt. Alternativ oder ergänzend können die Begriffe in einem einsprachigen Wörterbuch (z. B. *Oxford Advanced Learners' Dictionary,* Oxford 2000) nachgeschlagen und in die Besprechung eingebunden werden:

outpost – 1: a small military camp away from the main army, used for watching an enemy's movements, etc.
2: a small town or group of buildings in a lonely part of a country; e.g. the last outpost of civilization

progress – the process of improving or developing, or of getting closer to achieving or completing sth.

Tafelbild (Teil 1):

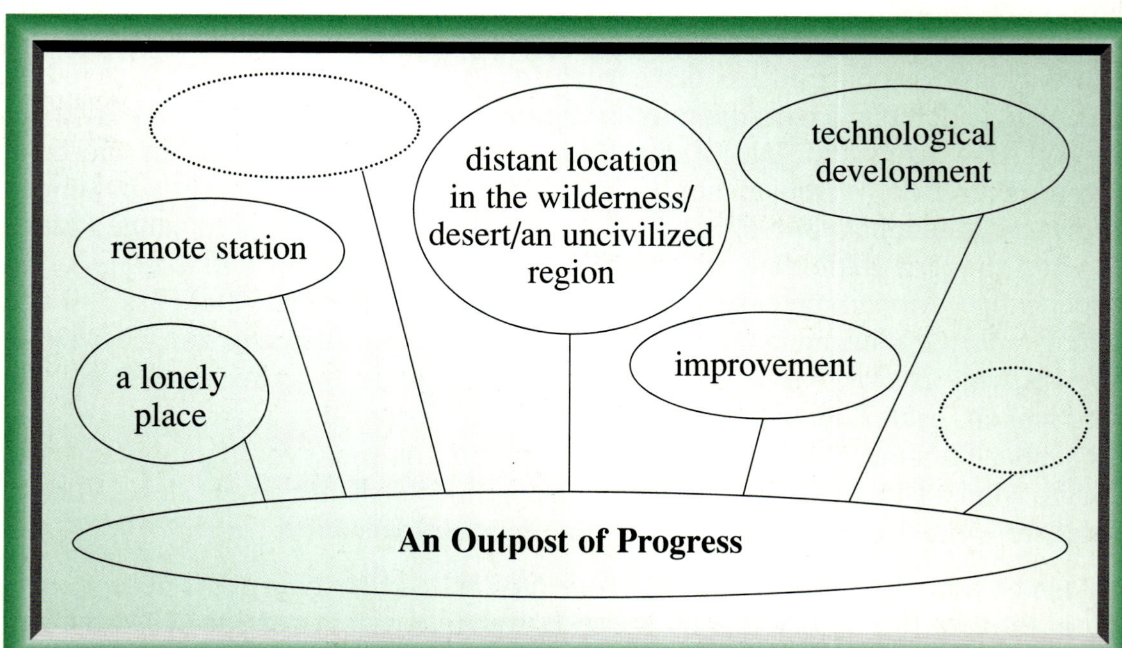

Nach der *brainstorming*-Phase wird konkreter auf die mögliche Thematik hingeführt und das Tafelbild ergänzt. Die gesamte Phase sollte zwar ohne viel Lehrerlenkung erfolgen, es ist aber auf einen zügigen Verlauf zu achten. Um Zeit zu sparen, kann der zweite Teil zunächst in Partnerarbeit in den Heften erstellt, dann im Plenum besprochen und von der Lehrperson an die Tafel gebracht werden:

Joseph Conrad placed his "outpost of progress" in some remote corner of the Congo. What effect might such an outpost have had on the region and its indigenous people?

Tafelbild (Teil 2):

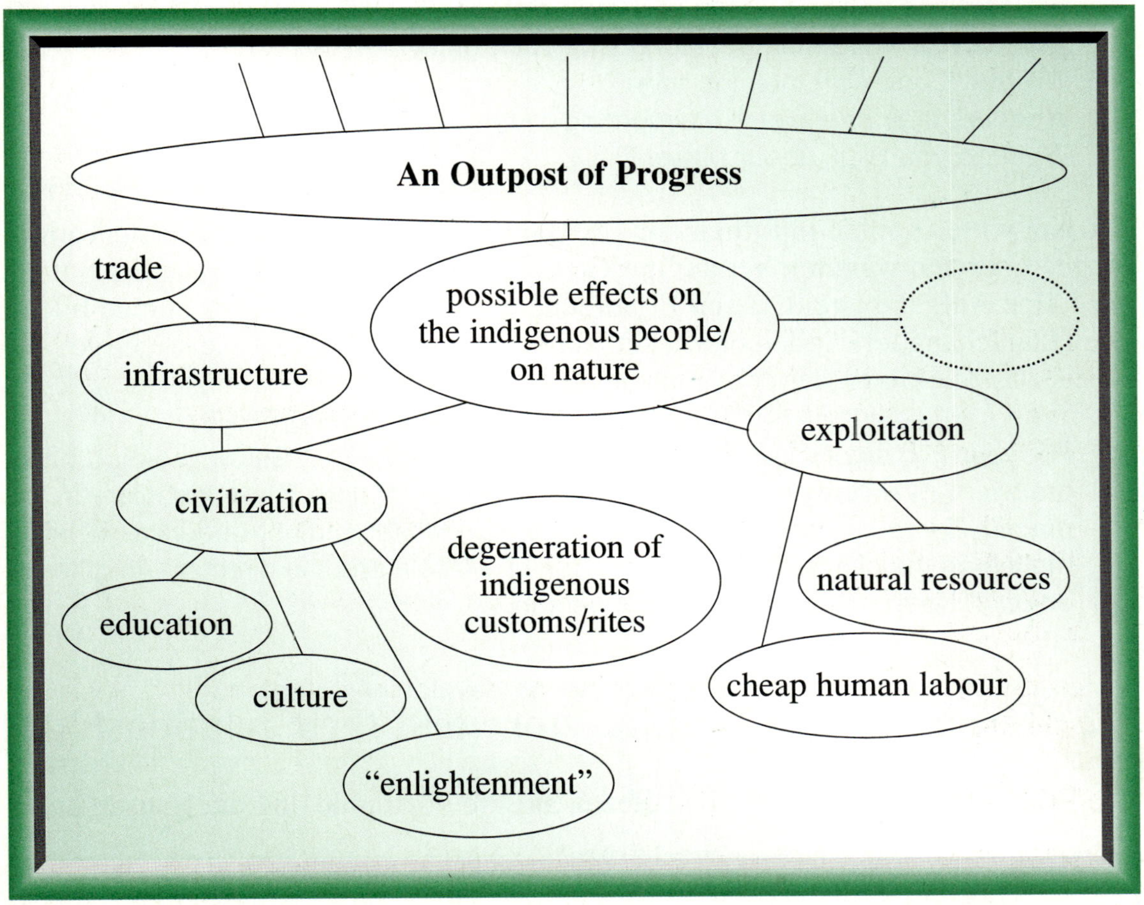

Bei der Besprechung können positive und negative Auswirkungen mit Plus- und Minuszeichen versehen werden. Welche Beiträge gebracht werden und wie kontrovers argumentiert wird, hängt davon ab, wie leistungsstark die Lerngruppe ist bzw. inwieweit in einem anderen Fach, z. B. Geographie oder Geschichte, bereits über den Kolonialismus und seine Auswirkungen gesprochen wurde.

Im Anschluss werden die ersten zwei Seiten der Geschichte gemeinsam gelesen (S. 6–7). Bevor Schülerinnen oder Schüler laut lesen, sollten sie zunächst Gelegenheit erhalten, den Abschnitt zu überfliegen *(skimming)* und die Vokabelangaben am Rand zu studieren. Die Aussprache einiger unbekannter oder schwieriger Wörter sollte von der Lehrperson bei Bedarf dem eigentlichen lauten Lesen vorangestellt werden.

Let's start reading together. First of all, skim the first two pages (6 and 7) up to the sentence: "'At any rate, I am rid of them for six months,' retorted the director." Check the vocabulary in the margin and prepare yourselves for reading aloud. You have three minutes!

Danach kann die Passage in vier kleineren Teilen gelesen werden, wobei noch keine inhaltlichen, sondern nur Fragen nach dem Vokabelverständnis geklärt werden sollten:

1. There were two men [...] on all the four sides, ll. 1–21;
2. There were three rooms [...] to play with, by and by, l. 22–p. 7, l. 7;
3. At any rate the director [...] We shall see, very soon, ll. 7–32;
4. Next day [...] I am rid of them for six months,' retorted the director, ll. 33–48.

Nach dem Lesen sollen sich die Schülerinnen und Schüler zum Verständnis und Eindruck des Textes äußern. Folgende Impulse können gegeben werden:

Who are the inhabitants of the "outpost of progress"?
What will life be like there at the trading station?
Will the two white men get along with each other?
Will they cope with their job there?
What are their chances like according to the director?
What do you think about Makola?

Die Antworten sollten mit direktem Textbezug (Zitate) erfolgen und erste Vermutungen über den weiteren Verlauf der Geschichte enthalten. Zum Ende der Stunde wird eine Aufgabe erteilt, deren Erledigung die Basis der nächsten Stunde bildet. Die Hauptcharaktere sollen erarbeitet werden. Zu Hause erfolgt die wichtige Vorarbeit, das Markieren der entsprechenden Textstellen:

For your homework, go on reading up to p. 11, l. 16 ("... Below the high bank, the silent river flowed on glittering and steady."). Check the vocabulary in the margin. Try to do without an extra dictionary. While reading, underline all information on the characters – Kayerts, Carlier, Makola and the director – in different colours. Keep one colour for each person.

1.2 The protagonists of the story and their relationship

Die Eröffnungsfrage nimmt direkt Bezug auf die Vorstunde und die Hausarbeit:

What do you think about Kayerts' and Carlier's success at the outpost now?

Die Schülerinnen und Schüler stellen fest, dass die anfängliche Euphorie der beiden bereits abgeflaut ist. Sie können prognostizieren, dass es den beiden wohl nicht viel anders gehen wird als ihrem Vorgänger. Nach dem Klassengespräch werden Gruppen zu maximal sechs Lernenden gebildet. Eine oder mehrere Gruppen sollen anhand ihrer Unterstreichungen (Hausarbeit) alle Informationen zu Kayerts bzw. Carlier sammeln. Makola und der Direktor werden zunächst ausgespart.

Zu erwartende Antworten und Schlüsselstellen im Text:

1. They get along with each other very well at the beginning of the story, like friends. They walk arm in arm, have a good time at the station and even after two months we are told that "the two men got on well together in the fellowship of their stupidity and laziness [...] And in time they came to feel something resembling affection for one another." (p. 10, ll. 11–15) The chief-assistant relationship is a relaxed one: "He [Kayerts] assumed his superiority jocularly, but his meaning was serious." (p. 8, ll. 46–47).

2. They are both like two lost boys taking on the challenge of adventure in that remote place believing in the illusion that they will do much better than their predecessor:
   - "They had been in this vast and dark country only a very short time, and as yet always in the midst of other white men, under the eye and guidance of their superiors." (p. 8, ll. 3 – 5)
   - "And now dull as they were […] they felt themselves very much alone, when suddenly left unassisted to face the wilderness […]." (p. 8, ll. 6 – 8)
   - "They were two perfectly insignificant and incapable individuals […]." (p. 8, ll. 10f.)
   - "Kayerts and Carlier walked arm in arm […]; and they had the same, not altogether unpleasant, sense of danger which one half suspects to be imaginary." (p. 8, ll. 32 – 35)
   - "The first day they were very active […]; resolved to settle down comfortably to their new life." (p. 9, ll. 14 – 17)

3. + 4. Both regret their old life (p. 10, l. 6):

Kayerts (p. 9, ll. 33ff.)	Carlier (p. 9, ll. 45ff.; p. 10, ll. 1ff.)
– had been in the Administration of the Telegraphs and knew how to express himself correctly. (3) – quit his job after 17 good years to earn the dowry for his daughter Melie (4) – his wife is dead (3) – his daughter is being brought up by his sisters (3) – had a lot of friends and was a sociable man who liked a good chat at a café (3) – misses his life as a government clerk (3)	– is an ex-non-commissioned officer of cavalry (3) – had left the army (3) – was a burden for the family because of his laziness and impudence (3) – squeezed money out of the family (3+4) – was forced by his brother-in-law to take the job with the Company (3+4) – had to accept because he was completely broke (3+4) – misses "the clink of sabre and spurs", the garrison towns and girls, his life as a soldier (3) – was evidently a much ill-used man (3+4)

5. They talk about the natives as if they were animals. (p. 10, l. 24 – p. 11, l. 12).

Die Lektüre des restlichen Teils 1 (S. 11, Z. 12 – S. 15) kann mit der Hausaufgabe verbunden werden:

Read up to the end of part 1 (p. 15). Write one of the letters, either

1. Kayerts writes a letter to Melie about his life at the outpost. Don't forget to ask about new developments as to a prospective engagement.

Or

2. Carlier writes to his sister. Don't forget to complain about his brother-in-law.

Erwartet wird, dass in beiden Briefen ein Rückblick auf die bisherigen Ereignisse gegeben wird, d. h. es könnte etwas zur Fahrt mit dem Dampfer erfunden werden, die Situation auf der Außenstelle wiedergegeben und dabei eine Beschreibung der Aussichten und Absichten sowie des bereits ansässigen Henry Price *alias* Makola gegeben werden. Es könnten Einladungen zu bzw. Warnungen vor einem Besuch ausgesprochen werden. Die beiden könnten auch reflektieren, warum sie von zu Hause weggegangen sind und ob es richtig war, das Angebot der *Great Civilizing Company* anzunehmen.

1.3 The antagonist Makola and the escalation of violence (1)

Die Stunde beginnt damit, dass sich je zwei (oder bis zu vier) Schülerinnen oder Schüler mit dem gleichen „Briefverfasser“ zusammensetzen und sich die Briefe (reihum) vorlesen. Dabei sollen sie auf Fehler, Auslassungen, gut gelungene Passagen etc. achten und ihre eigene Arbeit korrigieren bzw. ergänzen.

Read your homework to a partner who has written as the same person as you. Correct each other and improve your letter with the help of your partner. / Gather in groups of four with the same letter writer ...

Nach dieser schülerorientierten Phase können Sie nun je einen überarbeiteten Brief laut vorlesen lassen und im Plenum besprechen. Hier wird Gelegenheit gegeben, Fragen zu behandeln, die in der Partner- (oder Gruppen-)phase aufgetaucht sind. Idealerweise sollten dabei die sich anbahnenden Probleme anklingen und somit sollte ein Übergang zur Hauptthematik der Stunde möglich sein. Mithilfe der Folie *(Solution sheet 1)* und durch die häusliche Lektüre kann die Lerngruppe bereits absehen, dass auf die beiden *„dear fellows“* Probleme zukommen werden, mit denen sie unter Umständen nicht fertig werden. Makolas Rolle wird zunehmend wichtig. Hier kann auch auf die eingangs angefertigten Charakterisierungen zurückgegriffen werden. Zunächst sollen die Gründe für das drohende Scheitern gefunden werden.

What about the two "dear fellows" and their "quiet life" at the end of part 1? [Do you see any potential problems for them in the future? Why?]

Die Lerngruppe kann diese in vier Kategorien einteilen:

1. unterschiedliche Charaktere/Temperamente
2. verschiedene Motivation, die Stelle anzunehmen
3. beide sind ungeeignet für die Aufgabe
4. die äußeren Umstände und Makolas Rolle überfordern die beiden.

Die Antworten sollten sich auf folgende Zitate stützen und entsprechend individuelle Ergänzungen für die Tafel liefern:

1. Kayerts:
   "Kayerts was moved almost to tears by his director's kindness [...]" p. 7, ll. 21f.
   Carlier: "a much ill-used man" (p. 10 , l. 10)

2. (ergibt sich aus Vorgespräch)

3.

- Director's comment, p. 7, l. 39: "Look at those two imbeciles."
- Narrator's comment, p. 8, ll. 3–31; unfit, could only live on conditions of being machines, they did not know what use to make of their faculties, incapable of independent thought (p. 9, ll. 14–32); Together they did nothing [...] (p. 10, ll. 12–15); They lived like blind men [...] (p. 10, ll.16–22).

The relationship between Kayerts and Carlier

Kayerts and Carlier walked arm in arm drawing close to one another as children do in the dark […]. (p. 8, ll. 32–33)

Kayerts' thoughts on Carlier:	Carlier's thoughts on Kayerts:
The idea that he would, perhaps, have to bury Carlier and remain alone, gave him an inward shiver. He felt suddenly that this Carlier was more precious to him here, in the centre of Africa, than a brother could be anywhere else. (p. 8, l. 47–p. 9, l. 3)	That poor Kayerts; he is so fat and unhealthy. It would be awful if I had to bury him here. He is a man I respect. (p. 9, ll. 10–12)

Before they reached the verandah of their house they called one another "my dear fellow". (p. 9, ll. 12f.)

4.
- p. 8, ll. 3–31: They had been in this vast and dark country […];
- p. 10, ll. 16–24: They lived like blind men [...]; Even the brilliant sunshine disclosed nothing intelligible […];
- p. 11, ll. 22–24 : The two men understood nothing, cared for nothing […]; p. 13, ll. 4–15: The Company never provisions […];
- p. 13, ll. 17–46: Then, one morning, […] a knot of armed men came out of the forest and advanced towards the station;
- p. 14, ll. 11–15: They both, for the first time, became aware that they lived in conditions where the unusual may be dangerous […].

Problems for the "dear fellows"

1. Characters:
   Kayerts – a good-natured government clerk; rather obedient and sensible, caring but to be respected ⇒ **weaker than Carlier**
   Carlier – a moody, frustrated military man ⇒ **tougher than Kayerts**
2. Motivation for the Company's job:
   Kayerts: joined the Company deliberately to make money for his daughter's dowry; wants to be successful and **is interested** in the job.
   Carlier: is a good-for-nothing who was forced to accept the job by his brother-in-law. He has **no real interest** in the running of the station.
3. Suitability for the job:
   - they are "imbeciles"
   - **unfit**
   - like "blind men"
4. Living conditions:
   - feeling of loneliness in the "vast and dark country"
   - strange and incomprehensible wilderness around them brings them "trouble into the heart"
   - they have no sense for the magic and beauty of the nature around them
   - boring, lazy days with only some books to read and talk about
   - enjoy visits by Gobila and his women, who bring food provisions
   - suffer from bouts of fever
   - armed strangers appear and make their stay suddenly dangerous

Makolas Rolle hat sichtlich an Gewicht gewonnen. Als Hausarbeit soll dies erarbeitet werden:

What role does Makola play? For your homework, go through the text again and write about Makola's position at the outpost and his relationship with the two white men.

1.4 The antagonist Makola and the escalation of violence (2)

Zu Beginn der Stunde wird der Name „Makola" als Impuls entweder mitten auf die Tafel geschrieben oder für die spätere Arbeit besser als Folienschnipsel per Overheadprojektor an die Wand projiziert. Mithilfe der Kopiervorlage *(Solution sheet 2)* kann mit entsprechenden Folienschnipseln sukzessive verfahren werden, wobei aus den Hausarbeiten die bedeutsamen Aspekte aufgegriffen werden. Zunächst sollte eine Charakterisierung des mysteriösen und ironischerweise den beiden weißen Männern überlegenen Schwarzen erfolgen. Dabei sollte erwähnt werden, dass er länger als die beiden Weißen dort ist und eine Weile die Außenstelle selbst gut verwaltet hat. Er wird als verschlagener und intelligenter „Neger" dargestellt (taciturn and impenetrable, [...] pretended to keep a correct account, S. 6, Z. 14–18), der lesen und schreiben kann und sogar einige Fremdsprachenkenntnisse hat. Er stehe mit dem „Evil Spirit" im Bunde und so umgibt ihn der Hauch des Mysteriösen. Die Assoziation, er könne eine Art „Voodoo-Meister" sein, kommt auf im Zusammenhang mit dem Tod des ersten weißen Chefs, der an dem Fieber starb, an dem später auch Kayerts und Carlier erkranken werden.

Den zweiten Teil der Stunde bildet die gemeinsame Fortsetzung der Lektüre mit Rollenverteilung ab Teil 2 (S. 15) bis „We heard that shot last night" (S. 18, Z. 16–17). Die Schülerinnen und Schüler sollen ihr Textverständnis durch eine knappe Inhaltsangabe der Passage zeigen. Im Hinblick auf Makola kann nun das Schaubild vervollständigt werden.

Als Hausarbeit soll der Rest des Textes gelesen werden. Der konkrete Leseauftrag lautet, Makolas Rolle weiter zu beobachten mit dem Hinweis auf Kayerts aufkommendes Misstrauen: „Isn't this Makola very queer today?" (S. 15, Z. 7–8) und eine mündliche (oder schriftliche) Wiedergabe des Gelesenen als *short plot summary* wird erwartet.

Read the second part completely. You should be able to give a short summary of the plot of the story to its end. What about Makola's role in it?

1.5 Rewinding the story and analysing the structure

Die Stunde beginnt mit der Frage nach dem Ende der Geschichte und einem kurzen Gespräch darüber, inwieweit dieses den in der ersten Stunde geäußerten Erwartungen entspricht. Daran schließt sich das Einbringen der Hausarbeit an. Die Handlung des zweiten Teils soll zunächst unkommentiert und ohne Interpretation wiedergegeben werden. Nachdem ein oder zwei *summaries* gehört wurden, sollen die Schülerinnen und Schüler knapp den Grund für Kayerts' Tod benennen. Um die tatsächliche Entwicklung hin zum tragischen Ende strukturell zu erfassen, soll die Geschichte vom Ende her rekonstruiert werden. Dabei ergeben sich zehn Sinnabschnitte, die analysiert werden können. Zunächst sollen die Textpassagen in Stillarbeit gefunden und markiert werden. Sie werden dann in Partnerarbeit auf die Kernaussagen reduziert:

What steps lead up to the ending? Let's rewind the story and move from the ending to the beginning of the final tragedy. Mark the passages where you see a development. Do that alone now. Take ten minutes.

Nach der Vorgabezeit vergleichen und begründen die Schülerinnen und Schüler im Klassengespräch ihre Einteilungen. Sie sollten auf die zehn unten notierten Textpassagen kommen. Danach erhalten sie den Auftrag zur Partnerarbeit. Um die Ergebnissicherung schülerorientiert ablaufen zu lassen, kann an zehn Paare je eine nummerierte Folie ausgeteilt werden. Die Paare sollen auf die Folie ihre Kurzin-

Kayerts and Carlier

At the beginning of the story:

They are his bosses.

They feel superior to any black and native person.

Makola

"cherished in his innermost heart the worship of evil spirits"

"taciturn and impenetrable, despised the two white men"

"He got on very well with his god. Perhaps he [the Evil Spirit] had propitiated him by a promise of more white men to play with, by and by."
pp. 6–7

At the end of part 1 and in the course of part 2:

They depend existentially on him and his wife (armed strangers).

growing dependence

growing superiority

... is superior to them because of his machinations with the armed strangers

"This Makola is invaluable."

unbezahlbar

Thanks to his "slave deal" they can show the director that they can do their job successfully.

... is a much harder and better businessman: his deal with the slave hunters is a veritable success for the company

"This infamous Makola."

Kayerts and Carlier

formation zum entsprechenden Teil (*step 10, step 9,* etc.) notieren und später der Klasse am Overhead-Projektor ihre Auswahl- bzw. Kürzungskriterien (was wurde erwähnt, was nicht) kurz erläutern.

Work with your partner now and give each step a headline or summarise the main information in no more than three to five sentences.

Rewinding the story's second part:

- **Step 10**
  Kayerts has hung himself from the cross, shortly before the director reaches the station:
  - "A shriek inhuman [...] pierced like a sharp dart [...]" (p. 25, ll. 28ff.)
  - "And, irreverently, he was putting out a swollen tongue at his Managing Director." (p. 26, ll. 32–33)
- **Step 9**
  Kayerts is in a trance-like state after he has killed Carlier. He goes mad in the course of the night:
  - "Night came, and Kayerts sat unmoving on his chair." (p. 24, ll. 31ff.)
  - "He stood up [...] like that of a man who, waking from a trance, finds himself immured forever in a tomb. '*Help! ... My God!*'" (p. 25, ll. 24–27)
- **Step 8**
  After finding out that Carlier had been unarmed: Kayerts accepts Makola's suggestion that he should tell people that Carlier died of the fever.
  - "Then Makola appeared before him [...]" (p. 24, ll. 3ff.)
  - "And he went away slowly to his expectant wife, leaving the two white men alone on the verandah." (p. 24, ll. 29–30)
- **Step 7**
  Carlier accidentally gets shot by Kayerts when they collide violently while fighting and chasing one another around the place:
  - "All at once he heard the other push his chair back [...]" (p. 23, ll. 25ff.)
  - "He felt deadly sick, and stood for a time in profound darkness."(p. 24, ll. 2–3)
- **Step 6**
  Carlier attacks Kayerts and makes him dash to his room and get his revolver. Kayerts is in great pain because of his bad health and in panic because of his fear of never being in control of Carlier again. He is in agony:
  - "Carlier swung a stool." (p. 22, l. 19ff.)
  - "He was completely distracted [...] that death and life had in a moment become equally difficult and terrible." (p. 23, ll. 21–24)
- **Step 5**
  Carlier demands the safely-locked away sugar from Kayerts. Kayerts does not want to use it except for special occasions. Carlier becomes furious and rebels against Kayerts as his boss. Carlier starts a fight:
  - "One day after a lunch of boiled rice, Carlier put down his cup untasted, and said: '[...] Bring out that sugar, Kayerts!'" (p. 21, ll. 36ff.)
  - "'Hold your tongue. Go out of this room,' screamed Kayerts. 'I dismiss you – you scoundrel!'" (p. 22, ll. 17–18)
- **Step 4**
  The steamer has not come. Carlier and Kayerts are suffering from loneliness and their limited mobility since they do not dare to leave the station. The natives are angry and Gobila is not sending provisions anymore. They are getting bored and Carlier is growing irritable:

- "Days lengthened into weeks, then into months." (p. 20, ll. 24ff.)
- "When the two men spoke, they snarled; and their silences were bitter, as if tinged by the bitterness of their thoughts." (p. 21, ll. 33–35)

- **Step 3**
  Carlier lends Makola a helping hand with the ivory. Kayerts, who has condemned Makola for his deal with the slave traders, joins them. He agrees with Makola's and Carlier's argument that it was a necessary and exceptionally good business for the company. The only problem both see is that one of Gobila's men got killed and some of them were taken away with the other men:
  - "Next morning they saw Makola very busy [...]" (p. 19, ll. 6ff.)
  - "And out of the great silence [...] its very hopelessness [...] seemed to approach them nearer [...] to envelop them with a solicitude irresistible, familiar, and disgusting." (p. 20, ll. 19–23)
- **Step 2**
  Makola has arranged the abduction of the black station men. He warns Kayerts and Carlier to leave it all to him, and in the morning, the station hands have gone, one of Gobila's men has been killed, but there are six splendid tusks of ivory there. Kayerts and Carlier are very upset and curse Makola for his machinations:
  - "In the middle of the night, Carlier waking suddenly, heard a man shout loudly;" (p. 16, ll. 33ff.)
  - "Nobody knows what suffering or sacrifice mean – except, perhaps the victims of the mysterious purpose of these illusions." (p. 19, ll. 3–5)
- **Step 1**
  Makola asks Kayerts and Carlier if they want more ivory. He offers to arrange a deal for them with the bad men who catch women and children. Kayerts and Carlier agree and let Makola proceed. He wants them to let the station men have a party and to provide lots of palm wine to make them drunk.
  - "There were ten station men [...]." (p. 15, ll. 10ff.)
  - "Some men from Gobila's village had joined the station hands, and the entertainment was a great success." (p. 16, ll. 30–32)

Die Schülerinnen und Schüler sollen sich über den offensichtlich gewordenen Wandel Makolas vom *invaluable* (S. 16, Z. 47–48) zum *infamous* (S. 21, Z. 5) *fiend* (S. 17, Z. 42) äußern. Das Abhängigkeitsverhältnis wird im Tafelbild ergänzt oder nun als weiterer Folienteil aufgelegt. Die Lerngruppe wird im Rückblick feststellen, dass die Geschichte insgesamt eine Ironisierung des Kolonialismus ist.

Als Hausarbeit wird ausgehend von Makolas Überlegenheit und dem tragikomischen Ende der Geschichte die Frage nach der Bedeutung des Begriffes *progress* neu gestellt. Dazu sollen die Schülerinnen und Schüler den Text noch einmal auf alle Textstellen *skimmen,* in denen Ironie zum Ausdruck kommt:

So if Makola, the clever "brute", is really the master of the station and superior to the two white men, what is the "progress" that the whites supposedly have brought? For that, skim the text again for all ironic passages. Mark them for our next lesson.

1.6 Irony and narrator comments

Die Hausarbeit aus der vorangegangenen Stunde wird im Verlauf der Stunde eingebracht. Zu Beginn wird der Lerngruppe folgendes Zitat vorgestellt (*Info sheet 3*):

When Conrad learned that *An Outpost of Progress* […] would be printed in two instalments, he objected that its division would damage the cumulative effect of his ironic method: "I told the unspeakable idiots that the thing halved would be as ineffective as a dead scorpion. There will be a part without a sting – and the part with the sting – and being separated they will be both harmless and disgusting". (Letters, I, p. 320)

Nach Verständnisklärung soll zunächst der Behauptung, dass der „cumulative effect of the ironic method" bei einer Zweiteilung verloren ginge, verifiziert werden. Dazu werden die Schülerinnen und Schüler aufgefordert in Partnerarbeit die zu Hause markierten Textstellen zu vergleichen.
Sie sollten dabei folgende Textstellen gefunden haben und auf diese im anschließenden Klassengespräch argumentativ zurückgreifen, um Conrads Behauptung begründen zu können. Die Hauptaussagen werden in einem Tafelbild festgehalten (siehe S. 44):

Page	**Text**	**Meaning**
p. 6, ll. 1–4	There were two white men […] Kayerts […] was short and fat; Carlier […] with a large head […] thin legs.	Two figures of fun are sent as "delegates of progress" – they are ridiculous and physically unfit for the job.
p. 6, ll. 9ff.	He (Makola) spoke English and French […] beautiful hand […] understood book-keeping […] worship of evil spirits.	The two absolutely ill-educated whites meet a black "native" who is better educated than they are. (Later they need his help in translating and making ivory deals.)
p. 6, l. 29 + p. 18, ll. 24ff.	Description of Makola's family life versus the "untidy men" + Makola did not open the store; […] playing with his children. It was a touching picture. […]	Makola's private life is well-ordered and his family is prospering – the white men have problems at home and soon fall ill.
p. 6, ll. 29ff.	There was also another dwelling-place […] under a tall cross much out of the perpendicular, slept the man who had seen the beginning […] he had been at home, an unsuccessful painter […]	The cross, as the symbol of Christendom, is the symbol of death in the story. Even the first white chief of the station had been a loser and K. and C. will do no better.
p. 7, ll. 5ff.	He (Makola) got on very well with his god. […] a promise of more white men to play with.	Makola, the heathen, is superior in everything to the white men. Hidden criticism of the "Christian mission" can be detected here.
p. 7, ll. 7–13	At any rate the director of the Great Trading Compa-	The symbol of progress, the steamer, is described

When Conrad learned that "An Outpost of Progress" [...] would be printed in two instalments, he objected that its division would damage the cumulative effect of his ironic method: "I told the unspeakable idiots that the thing halved would be as ineffective as a dead scorpion. There will be a part without a sting – and the part with the sting – and being separated they will be both harmless and disgusting".

(Letters, I, p. 320)

Gai Fraser, in: The Cambridge Companion to Joseph Conrad, ed. by J.H. Stape, Cambridge, Cambridge University Press, 1996, p. 30

	ny, coming up in a steamer that resembled an enormous sardine box […].	in a rather derogatory manner, later on its unreliability will be fatal for K. and C.
p. 7, ll. 14ff.	The director was a man ruthless and efficient […].	K. does not recognise that the director thinks of them as "imbeciles" and does not give them the slightest chance to succeed. His emotional thankfulness is another sign of his naïvety.
p. 8, ll. 32ff.	Kayerts and Carlier walked arm in arm […] as children do in the dark […].	Pure irony – considering the violent ending of their "affectionate friendship". Describing them as "children" adds to the impression that they are totally unable to manage life at the station.
p. 9, ll. 14–32	The first day they were very active [...]. Society [...] had taken care of those two men, forbidding them all independent thought […]. They could only live on condition of being machines. […] both, through want of practice, incapable of independent thought.	Society is blamed for their incapability, as it has left them with existential deficits. Such a system will not work transferred to the "natives".
p. 10, ll. 11ff.	But the two men got on well together in the fellowship of their stupidity and laziness. [...] They lived like blind men [...].	Only fools can hold out there.
p. 11, ll. 13ff.	For days the two pioneers of trade and progress would look on their empty courtyard […].	Inefficiency is getting worse.
p. 11, ll. 18ff.	[…] the trading post […] lay in the eloquent silence of mute greatness. The two men understood nothing, cared for nothing […].	Trade is at a stand-still, climax of inefficiency is stylistically emphasised by an *oxymoron:* eloquent silence.
p. 11, ll. 29ff. – p. 12, ll. 1ff.	In the centre of Africa they made acquaintance of Richelieu […]. They also found some old copies of a home paper. […] discussed […] "Our Colonial	One point of climax as to the men's incapability and further showing the absurdity of the situation: the two pioneers of progress make literary "contacts"

	Expansion" […], and began to think better of themselves […]. "Kayerts and Carlier were the first civilized men to live in this very spot!"	and meet culture in the jungle *(Three Musketeers, Leatherstocking Tales, Father Goriot).* They fancy themselves as heroes of civilization, having learnt from an old copy on Colonialism what ideological role they are supposed to fulfil.
p. 12, ll. 8ff.	They seemed to forget their dead predecessor; but […] Carlier went out and replanted the cross firmly.	The cross is now erect again as if waiting for the next ones to be buried beneath it.
p. 12, ll. 16ff. + p. 20. l. 6ff.	(Description of Gobila:) Gobila's manner was paternal, and he seemed really to love all white men. […] Perhaps in time they would disappear into the earth as the first one […].	Gobila is described as the "sage native"; his observations and his admiration for the white men as almost god-like creatures adds much to the funny and ironic tone of the story.
p. 13, ll. 4–5	The Company never provisions the stations fully […].	Pure irony: the company is not able to provide for its own people, how then should civilization be maintained by it?
p. 15, ll. 10–41	There were ten station men […], having engaged themselves to the Company for six months (without having any idea of a month […]), had been serving the cause of progress […]. The two whites had practically very little control over them.	Pure irony: the men, who are supposed to be the supporters of progress are illiterates and are kept to their duty through intimidation not because of idealism or conviction.
p. 17, l. 5	Makola, a civilized nigger […].	This epithet turns out to be most ironic (see above).
p. 20, ll. 37ff.	Once Carlier shot a hippo in the river. […] Gobila's people secured the carcase. It was the occasion for a national holiday, but Carlier had a fit of rage, […] exterminating all the niggers before the country could be made habitable.	A further step in the ironic depiction of C.'s and K.'s inability to cope with their situation, yet they still foster the stubborn idea of being superior to the natives.
p. 21, l. 5	[…] "this infamous Makola".	Climax of irony as to Makola's role (from being "invaluable", p. 16, ll. 47–48).

p. 25, ll. 34ff.	Progress was calling to Kayerts from the river. Progress and civilization and all the virtues. […] it called him to return to that rubbish heap from which he had wandered away […].	Rather sarcastic passage with the allusion that the steamer is the "container" of progress (cf. above) and that K. has, in fact, not achieved the intended personal improvement.
p. 26, ll. 1ff.	Kayerts stood still. […] began to stumble towards it [the cross] […] the station bell rang in a tumultuous peal its answer to the impatient clamour of the steamer.	Even more sarcastic: the noise announcing the long awaited steamer is meant as a sound of relief for the station men as it means an end to their sufferings but for K. it is the death-knell that tolls and his relief will be the redemption provided by death.
p. 26, ll. 8–10	The Managing Director of the Great Civilizing Company (since we know that civilization follows trade) […].	Pre-stage of climax: open irony and derision. Note the change of name: The Great Trading Company (p. 7, l. 8) → Great Civilizing Company.
p. 26, ll. 24–32	[…] he [the director] faced Kayerts, who was hanging by a leather strap from the cross […]. And, irreverently, he was putting out a swollen tongue at his Managing Director.	Absolute climax of irony and sarcasm, reached by the combination of using the cross as a gallows and K. showing his tongue to the director, as if he wanted to say that he had finally got the "highest wisdom" (cf. p. 25, l.7) about the director as a misanthropic exploiter of humans and the negative realities of colonization. As such, he is a victim of the imperialist system, and at the same time, a sacrifice, as his death is a warning to others and to the trading company not to go on like this. On the other hand, however, the situation is also very ambiguous because K. has put himself in a clownesque, ridiculous situation, which shows that he had obviously gone mad.

Die Lerngruppe kann eine Steigerung der Ironisierung des Geschehens feststellen. Sie wird stichwortartig an der Tafel als Ergebnissicherung festgehalten, wobei die inhaltliche Ausfüllung im Gespräch stattgefunden hat und anhand der Markierungen von der Lerngruppe nachvollzogen werden kann:

Culmination of ironic effects in Joseph Conrad's *An Outpost of Progress*

There is a continuous build-up of irony as to the

- superiority of Makola, the black, vs. incapabilities of K. and C., the whites
- role of K. and C. as "god-like creatures"/ pioneers of progress for the natives
- idea of "good fellowship" or friendship
- Trading Company and the task of fostering civilization by creating trade stations since "civilization follows trade"
- meaning of the cross as a symbol of Christianity and redemption vs. the cult of Evil Spirits celebrated by the natives
- meaning of the steamer as an icon of progress

*Irony and a distant, omniscient narrator are used to depict the absurdity of the "benefits of progress by colonization"
→ the division of the story is a disturbance for the ironic effect, if the parts are read in this way with a greater temporal break
→ the "scorpion metaphor" depicts the situation poignantly

Neben der Ironie, die als Stilmittel benutzt wird, kann auch die distanzierte Erzählerhaltung thematisiert werden. Dazu dient die Anschlussfrage, deren Lösung dem Tafelbild stichwortartig zugefügt wird (*):

Where did you find all the ironic passages in the text?

They are to be found in the narrator's comments. The narrator uses irony to highlight the absurdity of the situation. He also often inserts longer passages of explanations or even philosophical asides on loneliness and fear, which makes it seem like he is observing the two men from a distance. He is omniscient and so the impression arises that the characters are his puppets on a string.

Im Hinblick auf die sich steigernde Ironie ist die Teilung der Geschichte tatsächlich nicht günstig und Conrads Skorpion-Metapher ist treffend. Um festzustellen, ob die Bedenken wegen eines Bruches bei einer Zweiteilung auch inhaltlich begründet waren, soll die Struktur der Geschichte untersucht werden. Dazu wird die Klasse in zwei Gruppen geteilt. Die Hausarbeit wird entsprechend arbeitsteilig ausgeführt. Die Schülerinnen und Schüler erhalten den Auftrag:

Group 1 is going to deal with Part 1, group 2 is going to deal with Part 2 of the story. Look for structural elements like the timing of events and suspense, and mark the position.

1.7 Plot structure

Die beiden Großgruppen werden nun in sich in kleinere Gruppen unterteilt. Sie erhalten die Arbeitsblätter *(Worksheet 4: A timeline of* An Outpost of Progress*)* und große Plakatpapiere oder ein Stück auf der Rückseite beschreibbare Tapete. Der größte Teil der Stunde wird mit der Erledigung der Aufgabe unter Zuhilfenahme der Hausarbeit verbracht. Nach ausreichend viel Zeit sollen die Plakate an die Wand gehängt werden. Zunächst werden die einzelnen Produkte korrigiert. Anschließend sind alle aufgefordert, Stellung zu den Strukturen zu nehmen, zu ergänzen etc. Unter Umständen wird eine neue, gemeinsame Struktur erstellt. Bei Zeitknappheit kann mit den Lösungsvorschlägen *(Solution sheet 5)* verglichen oder gearbeitet werden.

Bei der Auswertung sollte folgendes Ergebnis erzielt werden:
Conrad musste die Teilung akzeptieren, konnte sie zum Glück allerdings selbst vornehmen. Sie liegt auch der Textausgabe zugrunde. Die Schülerinnen und Schüler können aufgrund ihrer Ergebnisse erkennen, dass die Teilungsstelle gut gewählt ist. Sie setzt in einem retardierenden Moment ein. Die Spannung entsteht dadurch, dass zeitlich lange Perioden des Wartens mit kurzen, handlungsaktiven Höhepunkten wechseln. Ihre Verteilung ergibt sich aus der Anfertigung eines Strukturdiagramms, das die Analyse abrundet. Dieses kann auch als Hausarbeit angefertigt werden. Dabei sollten die Schülerinnen und Schüler ihre Kurven möglichst auf eine Folie zeichnen. Zum Vergleich kann die Abbildung *(Solution sheet 5)* als Folienkopie bei der Besprechung herangezogen werden.

In der nächsten Stunde soll eine Kommission bestehend aus Vertreterinnen und Vertretern der Handelsgesellschaft und der Polizei die Vorkommnisse auf der Außenstelle untersuchen. Deren Hauptgesprächspartner ist Makola.

1.8 An investigation

Gegebenenfalls wird zunächst das Strukturdiagramm der Handlung besprochen (siehe oben). Sollte dies schon erledigt sein, kann direkt mit der Vorbereitung des Rollenspiels begonnen werden.

> Imagine that a commission from the Trading Company and the police investigate the events on the outpost. Their main interest centres on Makola. He is a suspect. Let's perform their conversation and see what they find out.

Die Schülerinnen und Schüler werden in Gruppen eingeteilt. Mindestens fünf sollten zusammenarbeiten und das Gespräch entwickeln. Dabei sollen sie die Vorkommnisse im Buch rekapitulieren und aus Makolas Sicht berichten, wie es zu den beiden Todesfällen kommen konnte. Der Reiz besteht darin, dass Makola seine illegalen Geschäfte vertuschen muss, die Kommission ihn aber diesbezüglich in die Enge treiben kann.
Nach genügend Vorbereitungszeit (ca. 15 Minuten) kann eine Gruppe vorspielen. Bevor eine zweite präsentiert, sollten die Stärken und Schwächen der ersten Gruppe sowie die gröbsten sprachlichen Fehler besprochen worden sein. Auch die anderen Gruppen sollten nicht nur auf die vorgebrachten Argumente und deren Logik Rückmeldung erhalten, sondern generell auf ihr Vortragsverhalten. Dies kann für die sich gegebenenfalls anschließenden Referate nützlich sein.

A timeline of *An Outpost of Progress*

Tasks:

1. Draw the timeline on a big piece of paper and add the events in the course of the given time periods mentioned in the text.
2. What do the timelines tell you about the structure of the story? Transfer them into a graph showing the ups and downs in the level of tension in the story:

Part 1:

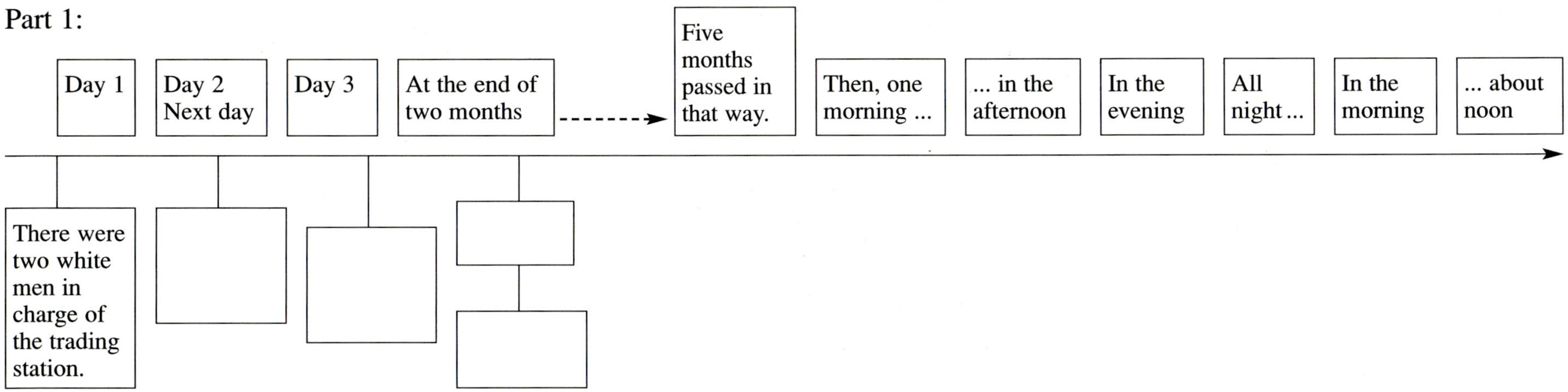

Part 2:

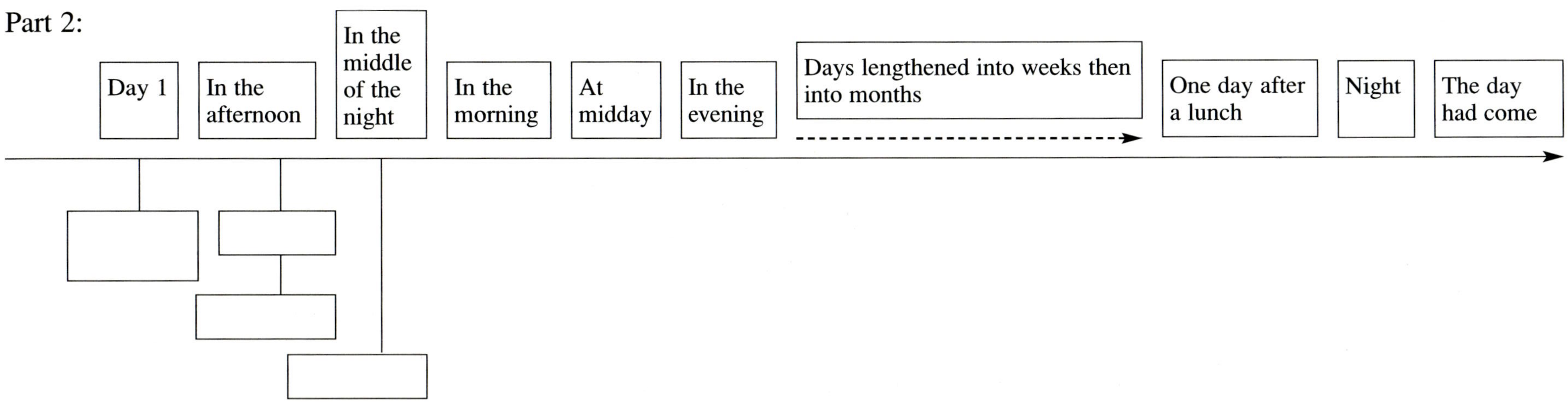

A timeline of *An Outpost of Progress* (Part 1)

- **Day 1**
  - There were two white men in charge of the trading station.
- **Day 2 Next day**
  - The steamer went off, not to return for another six months.
- **Day 3**
  - The first day they were very active.
- **At the end of two months** → **Five months passed in that way.**
  - "The two men got on well together [...] Together they did nothing [...] and enjoyed the sense of idleness for which they were paid."
    - "Such profitable visits were rare. For days the two pioneers of trade and progress would look on their empty courtyard in the [...] sunshine."
  - The two men understood nothing, cared for nothing but for the passage of days that separated them from the steamer's return.
    - At times Gobila came to see them.
  - "Now and then one of them had a bout of fever. It left them weaker, and their appearance changed for the worse. [...] they did not notice the change in their appearance, and in their dispositions."
- **Then, one morning ...**
  - "[...] a knot of armed men came out of the forest and advanced towards the station. [...] They both, for the first time, became aware that they lived in conditions where the unusual might be dangerous."
    - They became uneasy, went in and loaded their revolvers.
- **... in the afternoon**
  - The strangers left.
- **In the evening**
  - "[...] everything seemed so quiet and peaceful that they retired as usual."
- **All night ...**
  - "[...] they were disturbed by a lot of drumming in the villages [...]. They both thought they had heard shots fired during the night [...]."
- **In the morning**
  - Makola was gone.
- **... about noon**
  - "He [Makola] returned [...] with one of yesterday's strangers, [...]. Isn't that Makola very queer today?"

A timeline of *An Outpost of Progress* (Part 2)

Day 1
- "There were ten station men who had been left by the Director […]. The two whites had practically very little control over them."

In the afternoon
- "Makola came over […]."
- "Station in very bad order, sir. Director will growl. Better get a fine lot of ivory, then he will say nothing."

In thc middle of the night
- "Carlier, waking suddenly, heard a man shout loudly; then a shot was fired."
- "There are strange men about," […] "Never mind. I know," said Makola. "[…] Bring ivory […]."

In the morning
- "All the men gone last night!"
- "Will you come and look at the ivory […]?"

At midday
- "They hardly exchanged a word that day."

In the evening
- "The white men made a somewhat better meal. […] Slavery is an awful thing, stammered Kayerts."

Days lengthened into weeks, then into months
- "Gobila's people […] kept away from the station."
- "Stores were running short."
- "The steamer was late."
- "They had heard nothing from home for eight months."
- "Meantime [they] lived on rice boiled without salt, cursed the Company, all Africa, and the day they were born."
- "Carlier, undermined by fever, […] had become hoarse, sarcastic, and inclined to say unpleasant things."
- "Kayerts mooned about silently […]: His legs were swollen, and he could hardly walk."
- "They had long ago reckoned their percentages on trade, including that last deal […]. They had also concluded to say nothing about it [to the Director]."
- "The last fifteen lumps [of sugar] Kayerts had solemnly locked away."
- "They waited."
- "Days passed, silent, exasperating, and slow."

One day after a lunch
- "Bring out that sugar, Kayerts!"
- "Carlier swung a stool."
- "Kayerts snatched his revolver."
- "[…] they came into violent collision […]. A loud explosion took place."
- "Makola appeared […] Mr. Kayerts, he is dead."

Night
- "Kayerts sat unmoving in his chair […] with that kind of wrong-headed lucidity which may be observed in some lunatics."

The day had come
- "Kayerts […] stumbled out of the verandah, leaving the other man quite alone for the first time since they had been thrown there together."
- "Steamer! Steamer!"
- "The Managing Director […] landed first […] finding […] Kayerts, who was hanging by a leather strap from the cross. […] he was putting out a swollen tongue at his Managing Director."

Solution sheet 5

Structure of *An Outpost of Progress*

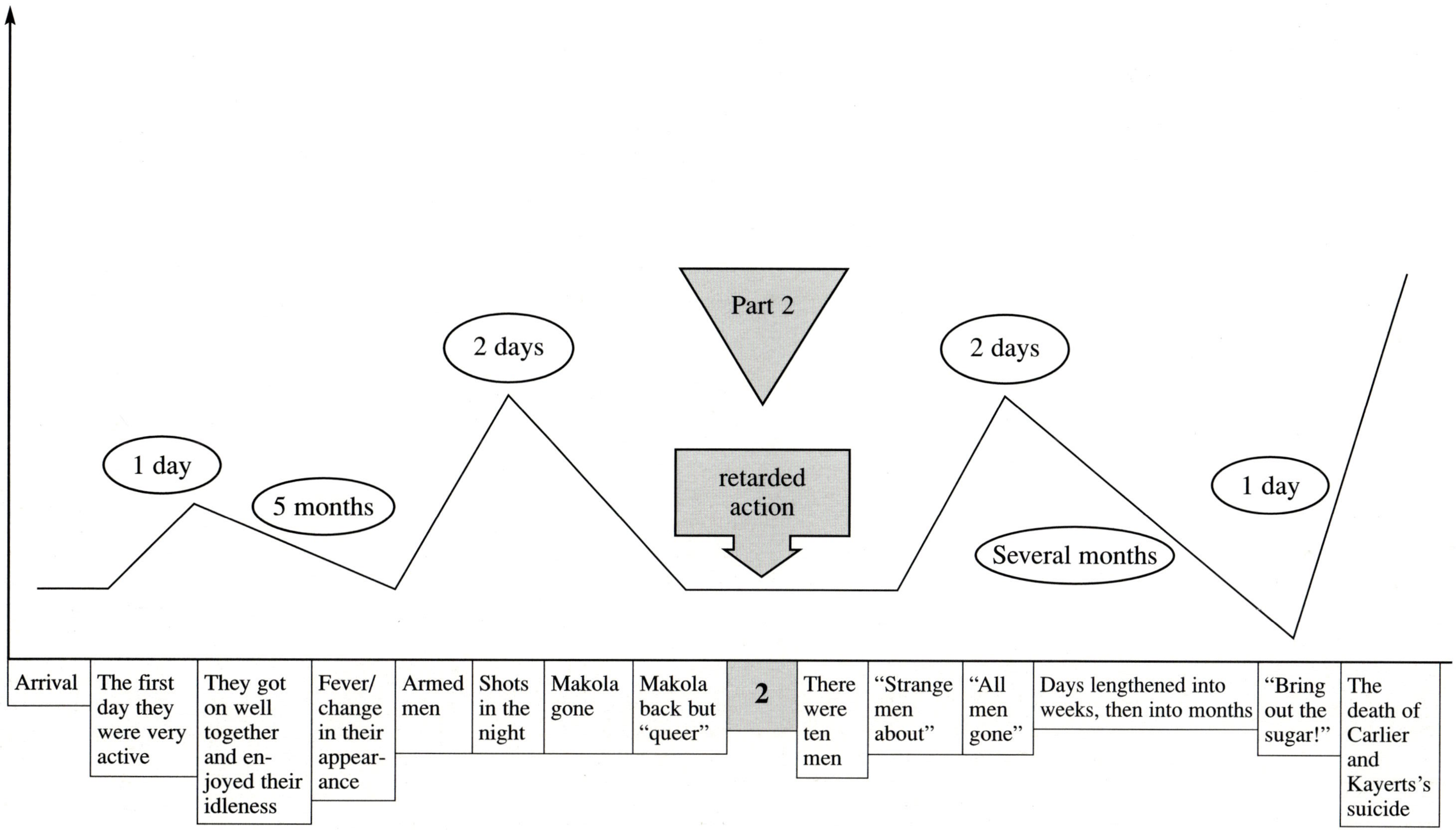

W. Somerset Maugham, *The Force of Circumstance* (1928)

1.9 Listening

Vor der eigentlichen Hörverstehensübung wird der erste Abschnitt der Erzählung (S. 26, Z. 34–S. 27, Z. 9) über CD (Track 1) präsentiert. Die Schülerinnen und Schüler erhalten den Arbeitsauftrag, auf die Gestaltung der Atmosphäre zu achten und diese mündlich in eigenen Worten wiederzugeben.

Listen to the CD. Pay special attention to the creation of the atmosphere. Then describe it in your own words.

Aufgrund der von Somerset Maugham gezeichneten Ausgangssituation werden die Schülerinnen und Schüler den Beginn der Erzählung vermutlich als düster und bedrohlich auffassen. Adjektive wie *gloomy, dangerous, threatening* sind daher als Ergebnisse zu erwarten.

In einem nächsten Schritt werden die Schülerinnen und Schüler dazu aufgefordert, ausgehend von der geleisteten Vorarbeit über den Inhalt der Erzählung zu spekulieren.

What might this short story be about? Speculate on its contents.

Entsprechend der oben diskutierten Ergebnisse sind auch hier Vorschläge zu erwarten, die von der eigentlichen Erzählung in erheblichem Maße abweichen. Die Gestaltung der Eingangspassage lässt weniger die Geschichte einer gescheiterten Beziehung als vielmehr den Bericht eines Abenteuers, einer Naturkatastrophe oder eines Aufstandes einheimischer Gruppierungen erwarten.

In diesem Zusammenhang sollten die Schülerinnen und Schüler auf die Rolle des Sembulu River aufmerksam gemacht werden, der sich leitmotivisch durch die ganze Erzählung zieht. Zu Beginn hat er „the white pallor of death“ (S. 26, Z. 39f.), ein Einheimischer kann sich mit seinem Boot kaum an der Oberfläche halten. Doris lernt Malaysia in Reisebeschreibungen als ein Land mit „great ominous rivers“ (S. 31, Z. 13) kennen und schließlich verlässt sie ihren Ehemann mit dem Boot „and the river was ghostly“ (S. 47, Z. 9). Der Fluss steht somit für die dunkle Welt des Dschungels, der die in seinen Bereich eindringende westliche Welt ständig bedroht und diejenigen verschlingt, die sich ihm – wie Guy – nicht zu entziehen wissen. Eine Koexistenz beider Sphären scheint nicht möglich, Doris wird das Land am Ende verlassen.

Im Anschluss an diese Einstiegsphase sollen die Schülerinnen und Schüler für die weitere Interpretation wichtige Informationen in einer Hörverstehensübung erarbeiten. Dazu werden die Ergebnisse in Einzelarbeit in ein Arbeitsblatt *(Worksheet 6)* eingetragen, auf das im weiteren Verlauf der Unterrichtseinheit rekurriert werden kann.

Die Schülerinnen und Schüler sollen sich zuerst mit den zu bearbeitenden Fragen vertraut machen. Danach werden die Textpassagen trackweise präsentiert. Nach dem Abspielen jeweils eines Tracks erhalten sie fünf Minuten Zeit, um ihre Antworten in Stichworten im Arbeitsblatt einzutragen.

William Somerset Maugham, *The Force of Circumstance* – Listening comprehension

Read the questions below carefully then listen to the CD. Don't write while you are listening. You'll be given five minutes after each track to fill in the required information. Keywords are **enough.**

1. **What do we learn about Guy?**

   looks: __________

   character: __________

2. **How did Guy and Doris meet?**

   when? __________

   where? __________

   how? __________

3. **Collect information on the situation of half-castes.**

   mothers: __________

   fathers: __________

   family situation: __________

   future: __________

4. **Describe the relationship between Guy and Doris.**

Read the worksheet carefully. I'll play the CD to you. Don't write while you are listening. You'll get about five minutes after each passage to fill in your answers in keywords.

Lösungen zu Worksheet 6:

1. What do we learn about Guy?

   looks:
   - twenty-nine years old
   - a little round man
   - red face
   - blue eyes
   - pimply
   - not Doris's type

   character:
   - cheery
   - still a schoolboy
   - gay, jolly
   - doesn't take anything seriously
   - constantly laughing
   - has got charm

2. How did Guy and Doris meet?

   when?
   - nine months ago

   where?
   - in Britain
   - at a small place by the seaside
   - at the same hotel

   how?
   - Guy is home on leave
   - Doris is on holiday with her mother
   - Guy asks Doris to marry her
   - Doris is determined to refuse him
   - she is overwhelmed by unexpected emotion and accepts him

3. Collect information on the situation of half-castes.

   mothers:
   - native women

   fathers:
   - British clerks or officers

   family situation:
   - while their parents live together they live in a sort of family
   - when their fathers have separated from their mothers they live with their mothers in the village and have no contact to their fathers

   future:
   - financially they are provided for
   - they get a good education and then work as clerks in government offices

4. Describe the relationship between Guy and Doris.

   - Guy loves Doris
   - they understand each other well
   - they are shy of displaying emotions
   - they talk to each other ironically
   - they don't usually embrace in the middle of the day

Im anschließenden Unterrichtsgespräch werden die Resultate verglichen und ergänzt.
Nachdem die Schülerinnen und Schüler gut ein Viertel der Erzählung über Hörverstehen zur Kenntnis genommen haben, erhalten sie den Arbeitsauftrag, die Geschichte aufgrund ihrer auf dem Arbeitsblatt gesammelten Ergebnisse zu Ende zu führen. Dabei soll lediglich das Handlungsgerüst schriftlich festgehalten werden. Die Ausarbeitung erfolgt mündlich.

Use the information on your worksheet to finish the story. Write down no more than the storyline.

Haben die Schülerinnen und Schüler das Handlungsgerüst ihrer Erzählungen fertiggestellt, werden sie aufgefordert im Klassenzimmer umherzugehen. Auf ein Zeichen des Lehrers wenden sich die Schülerinnen und Schüler den ihnen am nächsten stehenden Personen zu und erzählen sich gegenseitig ihre Geschichten anhand ihrer Notizen. Alternativ kann auch während des Umhergehens Musik eingespielt und als Signal an einer beliebigen Stelle abgebrochen werden.

Now get up and walk about the room. At my signal tell your story to the person next to you.

Diese Vorgehensweise ermöglicht es jedem Schüler und jeder Schülerin, die eigene Geschichte mindestens einmal zu erzählen. Der Vorgang kann wiederholt oder abgeändert werden. Als Variante kann im zweiten oder dritten Durchgang der Auftrag lauten:

Now tell the story that you have just been told to your new partner.

Der kommunikative Umsatz ist hoch, wobei entsprechende Zugeständnisse an die Fehlerhäufigkeit gemacht werden müssen. Als Hausaufgabe soll der Text fertig gelesen werden.

Read the complete text and pay special attention to Guy's relationship to the women.

1.10 Guy's relationships

Im Zentrum dieser Stunde stehen die Unterschiede in den Beziehungen Guys zu seiner Frau und seiner malayischen Lebensgefährtin. Die vorangegangene Stunde bot bereits Informationen zur ersten Begegnung von Guy und Doris sowie zur Situation der eingeborenen „Familien" weißer Kolonisten. Guy selbst gibt wichtige Einblicke in sein Privatleben, wenn er Doris von seiner Vergangenheit berichtet (S. 37, Z. 1–S. 39, Z. 36).
Die Schülerinnen und Schüler sollen zunächst in Partnerarbeit in dieser Passage wichtige Informationen zum Thema unterstreichen.

Read p. 37, l. 1 to p. 39, l. 36. Underline information on Guy's reasons for having a relationship with a Malay woman and on the relationship itself.

Im anschließenden Unterrichtsgespräch soll Guys Beziehung zu der Malayin mit seiner Beziehung zu Doris verglichen werden. Die Ergebnisse werden an der Tafel festgehalten:

Guy's relationships

<u>the Malay woman</u>	<u>Guy</u>	<u>Doris</u>
too young lonely desperate situation	reasons	in his late twenties looks for a wife fed up with the present
doesn't love her only a temporary arrangement	relationships	loves her marriage forever
'A lot of fellows have native wives [...].' (p. 30, ll. 7f.)	explanation	'I'd made up my mind to marry when I was home.' (p. 39, ll. 32f.)
sends her away	consequence	marries Doris

Im Anschluss an die Auseinandersetzung mit Guys Motiven soll die Situation der beiden Frauen aus ihrer eigenen Sicht analysiert werden. In Gruppen von vier Personen sammeln die Schülerinnen und Schüler zunächst Informationen zu der Malayin und zu Doris. Danach soll in den Gruppen die jeweilige Handlungsmotivation der beiden Frauen besprochen werden. Das Gruppenergebnis soll von einem oder zwei Gruppensprechern in einem mündlichen Statement vorgetragen werden. Die Ergebnisse dieser Gruppenarbeit werden an der Tafel festgehalten. Die folgenden Anweisungen sollten entweder über Folie präsentiert oder als *Task sheet (Tasks for teams: Doris and the Malay woman)* zum Mitlesen ausgeteilt werden.

So far we've been looking at the situation from Guy's point of view. Now we are going to concentrate on the situation as it presents itself to the two women. Work in groups of four.
Collect information on the Malay woman and on Doris, then discuss their respective behaviour.
Why does the Malay woman keep coming back to Guy's house?
Why does Doris leave Guy even though she doesn't blame him?
Choose one or two spokespersons from among your group and present the results of your discussion in an oral statement.

Tasks for teams: Doris and the Malay woman

Your task:

Collect information on the Malay woman and on Doris, then discuss their respective behaviour.

- Why does the Malay woman keep coming back to Guy's house?
- Why does Doris leave Guy even though she doesn't blame him?

Present!

- Choose one or two spokespersons from among your group and present your results in an oral statement.

Tasks for teams: Doris and the Malay woman

Your task:

Collect information on the Malay woman and on Doris, then discuss their respective behaviour.

- Why does the Malay woman keep coming back to Guy's house?
- Why does Doris leave Guy even though she doesn't blame him?

Present!

- Choose one or two spokespersons from among your group and present your results in an oral statement.

Tasks for teams: Doris and the Malay woman

Your task:

Collect information on the Malay woman and on Doris, then discuss their respective behaviour.

- Why does the Malay woman keep coming back to Guy's house?
- Why does Doris leave Guy even though she doesn't blame him?

Present!

- Choose one or two spokespersons from among your group and present your results in an oral statement.

Lösungen zu Task sheet 7:

The Malay woman's behaviour:
- keeps coming back to Guy's house
- makes scenes
- blackmails Guy
- tries to attract Doris's attention

Doris's behaviour:
- separates from Guy for six months
- Guy has to sleep in a separate room
- he mustn't touch her
- forgives him, doesn't blame him
- knows she is unreasonable
- feels nausea at the thought of Guy and the other woman
- leaves Guy for good

Oral statement on the women in W. Somerset Maugham, *The Force of Circumstance* (1928)
The Malay woman doesn't want to give up Guy. She has been living with Guy for ten years and she is the mother of his children. So she feels she, rather than the strange woman from England, has a right to be regarded as his wife. When Guy doesn't react to her attempts at winning him back, she tries – successfully – to attract Doris's attention. We do not know whether she loves Guy, but she certainly wants to go back to him and, in the end, she succeeds.
Doris's and Guy's relationship is not characterised by emotion or even passion. We get the impression of comradeship rather than love, although Guy tells Doris more than once that he loves her. When Doris learns about his relationship to another woman she does not blame him – after all, the relationship was over before Guy even met Doris. But she cannot continue living as his wife. She feels a physical repulsion at the mere thought of touching him or of him touching her. Having tried to overcome this for six months, she leaves Guy because she knows that things could never be the same as they were at the beginning of their relationship.
The gloomy setting of the first scene of the story foreshadows Doris's but also Guy's fate. In the end, they both have to give in to the hostile rules and requirements of reality.

Zur nächsten Stunde soll sich die Lerngruppe mit den Lebensbedingungen in den Kolonien ausgehend von Doris' Erfahrungen häuslich beschäftigen:

Underline passages in the text that give information on life in the colonies. Pay special attention to what we learn about Doris's life in the colonies.

1.11 What is the "force of circumstance"?

Zum Abschluss der Interpretation machen sich die Schülerinnen und Schüler ein Bild vom Leben in den britischen Kolonien zu Beginn des 20. Jahrhunderts. In Partnerarbeit sollen sie die in der häuslichen Vorbereitung markierten Passagen sammeln und in Kategorien einteilen.

Eine besondere Rolle kommt in diesem Zusammenhang Doris zu. Sie verkörpert die britische Lebensart und richtet Guys Wohnung nach westlichem Stil ein und bringt damit ein Stück europäische Kultur in die Kolonien (S. 32, Z. 6-14). Damit erfüllt Doris die traditionelle Rolle des Kulturträgers, die britische Frauen in den Kolonien einnahmen. (Vgl. hierzu Philip Holden, *Orienting Masculinity, Orienting Nation.* W. Somerset Maugham's Exotic Fiction, Westport, CT: Greenwood Press, 1996, S. 99)

Compare the results of your homework. Find different categories for grouping them.

Die Ergebnisse werden an der Tafel gesammelt.

Life in the colonies

1. **the country**:
   hot; melancholy; beautiful; open and wide; cheerful; many different animals; cloudless skies

2. **the natives**
   men:
   - work for the whites, mainly as servants
   - live in separate settlements
   - keep to themselves

   women:
   some of them have relationships and even children with white men

3. **the whites**
   men:
   - clerks or officers
   - work for trading companies or the government
   - form the upper class of society
   - often live in isolated outstations
   - primitive living conditions
   - suffer from loneliness
   - single men often take native wives and have children with them
   - they send these native families away when they get tired of them
   - no contact to other white people
   - mail can be sent or received only once a month

   women:
   - bring about and uphold a British lifestyle
   - represent "Englishness"

Nachdem Doris' Situation im Mittelpunkt der vorangegangen Besprechung stand, soll sie nun selbst zu Wort kommen. Eine Schülerin soll auf dem *hot seat* Auskunft darüber geben, warum sie Guy verlassen hat. Am Ende soll die Frage geklärt werden, was es mit der „force of circumstance" auf sich hat. Alternativ könnte auch der kreative Auftrag gegeben werden, als Doris einen Tagebucheintrag oder Brief nach England an eine alte Freundin zu verfassen, aus dem ersichtlich wird, warum sie so lange auf ihre Entscheidung warten ließ usw.

Die Schülerin, die sich hierfür bereit erklärt, wird von einer kleinen Gruppe unterstützt. Die anderen überlegen sich in Partnerarbeit Fragen, die sie Doris stellen könnten. Diese dürfen und sollen provokativ sein, z. B. ob sie Guy wirklich aus

Liebe geheiratet habe, warum sie so lange mit ihrer Entscheidung gewartet hatte, usw. Die Gruppe um die Schülerin präpariert die Kandidatin mit möglichen Antworten auf die zu erwartenden Fragen.

Let's ask Doris about her experiences and decision to leave Guy after all. We will need one person to play Doris. She will be prepared within a group of friends for defending herself against all the others. The rest of the class will work out good, provocative questions to tease the truth out of her. Work together with a partner.

Nach einer genügend langen Vorbereitungsphase kann die Aktivität beginnen. Die Schülerinnen und Schüler setzen noch einmal den Inhalt der Geschichte um und erfahren durch die Auseinandersetzung mit Doris' Motiven, weshalb es für sie geradezu ein „Sachzwang" ist, Guy zu verlassen. Die Vielschichtigkeit des Titels soll hierauf aufgedeckt werden.

Taking into consideration everything we have found out about Somerset Maugham's short story, try to explain its title.

In dem Unterrichtsgespräch soll deutlich werden, dass alle drei Hauptcharaktere den Mechanismen der herrschenden Gegebenheiten ausgeliefert sind. Guy, weil er sich – nicht fest in westlichen Traditionen verwurzelt – dem Einfluss des Dschungels nicht entziehen kann; die Malayin, weil sie sich zunächst für ihre Eltern und Geschwister, dann für ihre Kinder verantwortlich sieht; Doris, die Repräsentantin westlicher Kultur, weil für sie ein Kompromiss zwischen Zivilisation und „Chaos" nicht möglich ist.

Explanation of Title !

The Force of Circumstance

Guy	⇒	pressure of loneliness	⇒	lives with a Malay girl
Malay woman	⇒	poverty of her family	⇒	becomes Guy's mistress
Guy	⇒	pressure of society	⇒	marries a British girl
Doris	⇒	unexpected emotions	⇒	gets married to Guy
Malay woman	⇒	responsibility for her family	⇒	wants to go back to Guy
Doris	⇒	inexplicable emotions	⇒	leaves Guy
Guy	⇒	pressure of the situation	⇒	calls the Malay girl back

⇓

the force of circumstance

Abschließend kann die Gruppe darüber spekulieren, wie das Leben der beiden wohl weitergeht. Je nachdem, wie viel Zeit noch zur Verfügung steht, kann dies in einem gemeinsamen Gespräch geschehen oder in einer aufwändigeren Form (Partner- oder Gruppenarbeit, eventuell mit Auftrag eine Szene oder einen Dialog zu erfinden).
Als Hausarbeit, die auch zur Überleitung zu Orwells Essay dienen kann, sollen die Schülerinnen und Schüler anhand der Sammlung einen kurzen Text zum Thema „White Life in the Colonies" verfassen.

Use the information that you have just collected to write a short essay on "White Life in the Colonies".

White Life in the Colonies

In the days of colonialism, Asia was a beautiful, but more or less unknown, country.

White people usually did not go there to settle and stay forever. They went there because they were offered good jobs or hoped to make money. They either worked as clerks for private enterprises or the administration or they were soldiers. Even if they were born in the country and knew its language and its people, like Guy in Somerset Maugham's story, they kept to themselves and were careful not to become too intimate with the natives because they formed the upper class of colonial society.

Those natives who were in contact with white people usually worked as their servants. The local nobility often entertained relationships with the whites that yielded profit for both sides.

Many whites had to live in isolated outstations, where they had little or no direct contact to other white people. Visitors were rare and the mail came about once a month. This meant that information about the "outside world" was scarce and – when it arrived – outdated. To relieve their loneliness, some of the white men took native wives and even had children with them but didn't really see them as their families. The responsibility for those native families ended with a small allowance for the women and the payment of the school fees for the sons. The role of white women was to bring the British lifestyle to the colonies. They guaranteed the survival of colonial values in a hostile native world.

Notizen:

George Orwell, *Shooting an Elephant* (1936)

1.12 Pre-reading activities

Der Titel der *short story* könnte vermuten lassen, dass es sich um ein Ereignis bei der Großwildjagd handelt. Wenn die Schülerinnen und Schüler allerdings aufgefordert werden, das Bild des Arbeitselefanten auf den *Getting started*-Seiten in der Textausgabe hinzuzuziehen, dann kann mit der Frage:

- Why should one want to shoot such an elephant?

über den Inhalt spekuliert werden.

Orwells autobiografischer Essay, in dem das dilettantische, qualvolle Töten eines Elefanten durch einen jungen, von den äußeren Umständen bedrängten britischen Polizeioffizier beschrieben wird, ist durch die Ich-Erzählform ungemein dicht und ergreifend. Um die Wirkung zu vermitteln, sollte der Text ganz von der CD gespielt werden. Die Lerngruppe soll dabei still mitlesen. Das Vokabular in den Randspalten ermöglicht sofortiges Textverständnis. Nach dem Anhören sollen die Schülerinnen und Schüler spontan ihre Eindrücke äußern. Sie werden die Verhaltensweise des Offiziers ablehnen oder verteidigen. Die klassische Frage im Anschluss

- What is the essay about?

wird die folgenden drei thematischen Komplexe ergeben:

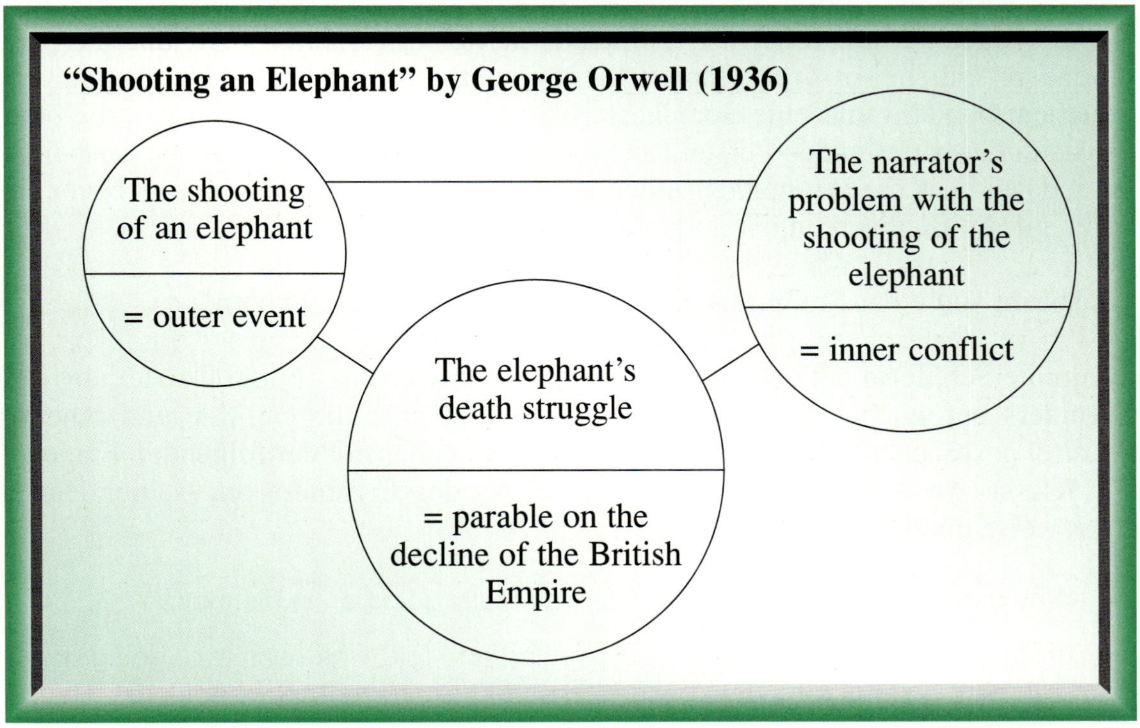

Obwohl Orwell ein tatsächlich selbst erlebtes Ereignis beschreibt, sollten die Schülerinnen und Schüler dazu angehalten werden, von dem Erzähler zu sprechen und diesen nicht mit Orwell gleichzusetzen.

In der nächsten Stunde soll zunächst das äußere Geschehen, das Töten des Amok gelaufenen Elefanten, in Form eines Streitgespräches zwischen dem Elefantenbesitzer, dem Erzähler und den erwähnten jungen und älteren Europäern (S. 54, Z. 35–48) erarbeitet werden. Die Hausaufgabe dient der Vorbereitung:

Write down five substantial arguments for each of the participants of a hot discussion about the shooting of the elephant:
1. the narrator; 2. the owner of the elephant; 3. a young European; 4. an old European.
Use information from the whole text for your line of argumentation.

1.13 Role-play

Die Lerngruppe erhält zunächst Gelegenheit, ihre häuslich erarbeiteten Argumente zu vergleichen und zu ergänzen. Nach fünf Minuten wird die Klasse aufgefordert, einen Stuhlkreis zu bilden. Es werden vorgefertigte Rollenkarten ausgegeben *(Task sheet 8)*. Der Zufall entscheidet so, wer als eine der Personen aktiv sein oder wer als Beobachter einer bestimmten Person fungieren wird. Die Beobachter setzen sich der zu beobachtenden Person gegenüber. Die Hauptakteure oder -akteurinnen setzen sich nach innen in den Kreis und beginnen unter Anmoderation der Lehrperson ihr Streitgespräch.

Nach ca. zehn Minuten werden die Hauptakteure zunächst nach ihrem Befinden gefragt:

How did you feel there sitting in the circle?

Danach sollen die Beobachterinnen und Beobachter ihre Kommentare gemäß den Anweisungen auf den Karten (Argumentationsweise, Verhalten gegenüber den anderen, sprachliche Ausdrucksfähigkeit etc.) innerhalb ihrer Beobachtergruppe vergleichen, bündeln und eine Sprecherin oder einen Sprecher bestimmen, die oder der dann der betreffenden Person Rückmeldung gibt. Die Abstimmungsphase dient auch dazu, dass die Hauptakteurinnen und -akteure eine Pause erhalten, bevor sie dann auf die Beobachtungen reagieren.

Insgesamt sollte der Stuhlkreis nicht länger als 20 Minuten dauern.

Wenn die Schülerin oder der Schüler die Rollenanweisung für die Darstellung des Erzählers befolgt hat, so sollte sie oder er nicht über die Gefühle und inneren Zweifel gesprochen haben. Die Lehrperson kann daher mit der folgenden Frage an die Klasse zur Analyse des inneren Konflikts des Erzählers und seiner Handlungsweise überleiten:

Why didn't the officer mention what was really going on in his mind?

Probably he felt if he had spoken his mind and told what was truly going on inside him, he would have exposed himself as a coward and a defeatist. He did not want to reveal his personal weaknesses and insecurities in that situation where he had to protect his position as a representative of the British colonial empire. He felt ashamed of telling them that he had at first been afraid of the elephant as it had run amok. However, it would have been even more embarrassing for him to admit his fear of the crowd of jostling Burmans. He had given

Task sheet 8

Role cards for *Shooting an Elephant* by George Orwell

Owner of the elephant

Sub-divisional police officer (narrator)

Young European

Old European

Observer of the owner of the elephant
Your task:

✍ Note down comments on the owner's:
- line of argumentation (logical, convincing statements)
- way of expressing himself (fluently or rather poor)
- behaviour (polite/rude; self-confident/self-conscious)

Give feedback to him or her but do it politely and with some positive remarks or some good advice.

Observer of the police officer (narrator)
Your task:

✍ Note down comments on the officer's:
- line of argumentation (logical, convincing statements)
- way of expressing himself (fluently or rather poor)
- behaviour (polite/rude; self-confident/self-conscious)

Give feedback to him or her but do it politely and with some positive remarks or some good advice.

Observer of the young European
Your task:

✍ Note down comments on the young European's:
- line of argumentation (logical, convincing statements)
- way of expressing himself (fluently or rather poor)
- behaviour (polite/rude; self-confident/self-conscious)

Give feedback to him or her but do it politely and with some positive remarks or some good advice.

Observer of the old European
Your task:

✍ Note down comments on the old European's:
- line of argumentation (logical, convincing statements)
- way of expressing himself (fluently or rather poor)
- behaviour (polite/rude; self-confident/self-conscious)

Give feedback to him or her but do it politely and with some positive remarks or some good advice.

in to the pressure of those he should have had under control. Never would he have let it be known that they had had the power over him to make him act against his conviction and will.

How come the pressure had such an effect on the narrator?

Der Erzähler hat unter dem Druck der Menschenmenge seine natürliche Tötungshemmung verloren. Die Schilderung der Stresssituation macht die Spannung in der Geschichte aus. Es treffen mehrere Faktoren zusammen, die die Schülerinnen und Schüler nach gemeinsamer Vergegenwärtigung des inneren Zwiespalts des Erzählers aus dem Text erarbeiten sollen.

Let's first have a close look at the situation and the narrator's inner conflict (pp. 51–52).

Zunächst wird der Ablauf im fragend-entwickelnden Unterrichtsgespräch rekapituliert und an der Tafel festgehalten:

The narrator's inner conflict under the pressure of the crowd

He had no intention of shooting the elephant. (p. 51, ll. 20–21)

They had seen the rifle [...]. It was a bit of fun to them [...], they wanted the meat. (p. 51, ll. 14–20) → He was looking and feeling like a fool. (p. 51, ll. 23–24)

↓

He saw the elephant and knew with perfect certainty that he ought not to shoot him. (p. 51, ll. 34–35)

↓

He did not in the least want to shoot him. He decided that he would watch him for a little while to make sure that he did not turn savage again, and then go home. (p. 51, ll. 44–46)

↑ impact of the crowd

"But at that moment I glanced at the crowd [...] an immense crowd, two thousand at the least and growing every minute [...] And suddenly I realized that I should have to shoot the elephant after all. The people expected it of me and I had got to do it; I could feel their two thousand wills pressing me forward, irresistibly." (p. 51, l. 47–p. 52, l. 11)

Danach soll die Lerngruppe die Hintergründe für die psychische Lage des Erzählers herausfinden. Dazu wird sie angewiesen in Partnerarbeit folgende Aufgabe zu erledigen:

Why did he feel the pressure so strongly?
Collect information about the narrator's state of mind. Focus on the historical, social and psychological factors that lead to his behaviour. Put your findings down in a table. Go through pages 48–49.

Ein Raster kann vorgegeben werden:

Factors contributing to the narrator's state of mind	
Socio-historical situation ...	Psychological situation ...

Für die spätere Besprechung beauftragt man ein Partnerpaar seine Ergebnisse auf einer Folie gut lesbar aufzuschreiben, die Textstellen anzugeben (Seite/Zeile) und sie dann vorzustellen.

Zu den Ergebnissen siehe *Solution sheet 9*. Diese Vorlage für eine Folie kann im Aufdeckverfahren benutzt werden, z. B. am Anfang, falls ein gemeinsamer Einstieg in die Aufgabe nötig sein sollte.

Als Hausarbeit sollen sich die Schülerinnen und Schüler vorstellen, dass sie als bester Freund oder beste Freundin des Erzählers den Essay als Brief erhalten haben. Was würden sie dem Erzähler zurückschreiben?

Imagine this story was sent to you by your best friend. What would you reply? Write a letter commenting on the shooting of the elephant and the narrator's confession at the end of the story:
"And afterwards I was very glad that the coolie had been killed [...]. I often wondered whether any of the others grasped that I had done it solely to avoid looking a fool." (p. 54, ll. 44 – 48)

Hinweise zur Lösung:

Der Erzähler offenbart, dass es ihm nicht um das Leben des Coolies oder eventuell weiterer Opfer ging. Er wollte nur nicht zeigen, dass er vor dem großen Tier einerseits Angst hatte, allerdings zugleich so sehr beeindruckt war, dass der „Unfall" für ihn gar keine Bedeutung mehr hatte. Er hat ein schlechtes Gewissen, das Tier entgegen seiner Absicht und Überzeugung getötet zu haben. Dass ihn die Einheimischen dazu gebracht haben, verzeiht er sich nicht. Die Schülerinnen und Schüler könnten im Brief erörtern, ob er sich denn tatsächlich lächerlich gemacht hätte, wenn er den Elefanten nicht erschossen hätte. Der Erzähler könnte auch gefragt werden, ob er den Elefanten hätte leben lassen wollen, wenn er einen Weißen getötet hätte. Es ist zu überlegen, ob der Erzähler das Drängen und die Rufe der Masse nicht subjektiv als Aufforderung, sich mutig zu zeigen, fehl- oder überinterpretiert hat.

Die Frage, wieso er sich lächerlich vorkommt und befürchtet, seine Souveränität einzubüßen, wenn er gegen einen gefährlich gewordenen Elefanten seine Waffe zieht, soll im anschließenden Verlauf erörtert werden.

The narrator's state of mind

Factors contributing to the narrator's state of mind	
<u>Socio-historical situation</u> (p. 48, l. 33 – p. 49, l. 9) – He was part of the imperialist system of the British Empire in the 1930s and had to fulfil his duty as a sub-divisional police officer in Burma. – As a European in Lower Burma, he was a victim of the anti-European feeling of the natives who had developed subtle and humiliating methods to undermine their oppressors without running the risk of being legally charged.	<u>Psychological situation</u> (p. 49, ll. 5 – 37) – The situation got badly on his nerves. – All that was perplexing and upsetting him. – He had already made up his mind that imperialism was an evil thing. – He wanted to "chuck" his job and get out of it. – He was all for the Burmese and all against their oppressors. – He bitterly hated the job he was doing. – He saw the dirty work of Empire at close quarters and all that oppressed him with an intolerable sense of guilt. – He could get nothing into perspective. – He was young and ill-educated. – He had to keep his problems secret ("the utter silence that is imposed on every Englishman in the East" p. 49; ll. 24 – 25). – He felt pity for the natives on the one hand, but on the other hand, also had sadistic feelings of taking revenge for being humiliated.
= strained co-existence of Burmese and Europeans	**= role conflict of the narrator**

1.14 The *pukka sahib code*

Zu Beginn der Stunde sollten zwei bis drei Briefe der Hausarbeit vorgelesen und besprochen werden (siehe Aufgabe oben). Im Anschluss wird die Frage im Raum stehen, warum sich der Erzähler so sehr mit der Angst trägt, sich der Lächerlichkeit preiszugeben.

Why is the narrator so afraid of making a fool of himself?

Besides being young and feeling odd in the extraordinary situation as a British officer and representative of the Empire, he is trained to keep to principles like "A white man mustn't be frightened in front of 'natives'" (p. 53, ll. 13-15). He also explains that his "whole life, every white man's life in the East, was one long struggle not to be laughed at" (p. 52, ll. 32 – 34).

Um den Schülerinnen und Schülern den mentalen Konflikt des Erzählers, der sich als Rollenkonflikt entpuppt, näher zu bringen, lohnt sich das Einbringen einer elementaren Zusatzinformation zum Selbstverständnis der damaligen Kolonialisten und ihrer Rolle als „Sahib". Um den psychischen „Überbau" des Erzählers anschaulicher zu machen, führt die Lehrperson den Begriff des „pukka sahib code" ein. Aus der Erklärung ergibt sich, dass die britischen Armeebediensteten schon durch ihre Erziehung an den englischen Colleges die Verhaltensregeln für „vorbildliche Kolonialherren" verinnerlicht hatten:

Pukka Sahib Code
The pukka sahib code guaranteed the functioning of the system and mechanisms of colonial imperialism by impressing the natives with the idea that no other country could rule them better than Britain. Emotions and doubts had to be suppressed:
"A stiff upper lip was nearly as important as 'grit', the sheer obstinacy of 'moral force'. Emotion was as destructive of the mystique as indecision".[1]
This code of behaviour was a mixture of the ten commandments and the poem "If ..." written by Rudyard Kipling. To permanently remind the members of the colonial society of their duty to behave according to the code, the ten commandments and the poem were inscribed on the wings of altars in colonial army churches.

Der Erklärung folgt das Austeilen von *Info sheet 10*. Gleichzeitig kann das auf Folie kopierte Blatt mit dem Overheadprojektor projiziert werden, um den Eindruck des Altars zu simulieren. Bei Zeitknappheit kann die deutsche Übersetzung zu Hilfe genommen werden *(Info sheet 11)*. Ziel ist es nicht, das Gedicht bis ins Detail zu analysieren, sondern zu veranschaulichen, mit welchen Mitteln die Psyche der Kolonialisten auf ihre Vorherrschaftsrolle vorbereitet wurde. Die Schülerinnen und Schüler sollen anschließend den *„pukka sahib code"* in eigenen Worten umschreiben. Als Ergebnissicherung könnte folgender Tafelanschrieb während des Gesprächs entwickelt werden:

1 zitiert nach: Schemann, Michael: Imperialismus im Werk George Orwells, Frankfurt am Main, Peter Lang, 1999, S. 99.

The Ten Commandments[1]

1. You shall have no other gods.
2. You shall not make for yourselves an idol before me.
3. You shall not misuse the name of the Lord your God.
4. Remember the Sabbath day by keeping it holy.
5. Honour your father and your mother.
6. You shall not murder.
7. You shall not commit adultery.
8. You shall not steal.
9. You shall not give false testimony against your neighbour.
10. You shall not covet.

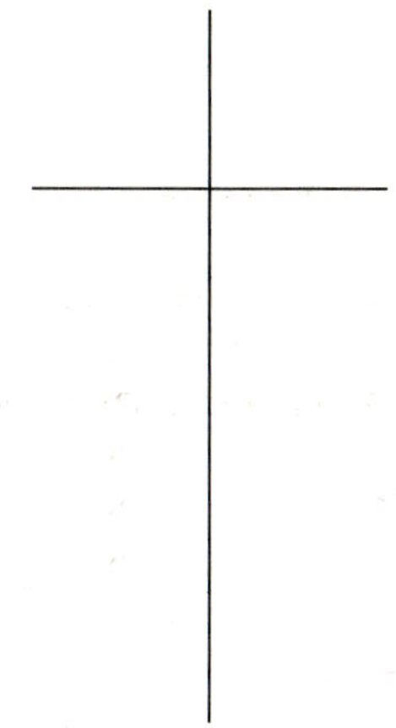

Rudyard Kipling: If …

If you can keep your head, when all about you
Are losing theirs and blaming it on you,
If you can trust yourself when all men doubt you,
But make allowance for their doubting too;
If you can wait and not be tired by waiting,
Or being lied about don't deal in lies.
Or being hated don't give way to hating,
And yet don't look too good, nor talk too wise;
If you can dream – and not make dreams your master;
If you can think – and not make thoughts your aim;
If you can meet with Triumph and Disaster
And treat those two impostors just the same;
If you can bear to hear the truth you've spoken
Twisted by knaves to make a trap for fools,
Or watch the things you gave your life to, broken,
And stoop and build 'em up with worn-out tools;
If you can make one heap with all your winnings
And risk it on one turn of pitch-and-toss,
And lose, and start again at your beginnings
And never breathe a word about your loss;
If you can force your heart and nerve and sinew
To serve your turn long after they are gone,
And so hold on when there is nothing in you
Except the will which says to them: "Hold on!"
If you can talk with crowds and keep your virtue,
Or walk with kings – nor lose the common touch,
If neither foes nor loving friends can hurt you,
If all men count with you but none too much;
If you can fill the unforgiving minute
With sixty seconds' worth of distance run,
Yours is the Earth and everything that's in it,
And – which is more – you'll be a Man, my son!

From: Rudyard Kipling: Rewards and Fairies, London, 1960, p. 175f.

[1] New International Version

Rudyard Kipling: If …

If you can keep your head, when all about you
Are losing theirs and blaming it on you;
If you can trust yourself when all men doubt you,
But make allowance for their doubting too;
If you can wait and not be tired by waiting,
Or being lied about don't deal in lies.
Or being hated don't give way to hating,
And yet don't look too good, nor talk too wise;
If you can dream – and not make dreams your master;
If you can think – and not make thoughts your aim;
If you can meet with Triumph and Disaster
And treat those two impostors just the same;
If you can bear to hear the truth you've spoken
Twisted by knaves to make a trap for fools,
Or watch the things you gave your life to, broken,
And stoop and build 'em up with worn-out tools;
If you can make one heap with all your winnings
And risk it on one turn of pitch-and-toss,
And lose, and start again at your beginnings
And never breathe a word about your loss;
If you can force your heart and nerve and sinew
To serve your turn long after they are gone,
And so hold on when there is nothing in you
Except the will which says to them: "Hold on!"
If you can talk with crowds and keep your virtue,
Or walk with kings – nor lose the common touch,
If neither foes nor loving friends can hurt you,
If all men count with you but none too much;
If you can fill the unforgiving minute
With sixty seconds' worth of distance run,
Yours is the Earth and everything that's in it,
And – which is more – you'll be a Man, my son!

From: Rudyard Kipling: Rewards and Fairies, London, 1960, p. 175f.

Wenn du den Kopf bewahrst und alle
um dich ihren verlieren und dir die Schuld geben,
wenn du auf dich vertraust, wenn alle an dir zweifeln,
doch ihre Zweifel geduldig zulässt,
wenn du warten kannst und nicht dabei ermüdest,
oder belogen wirst, so lüge nicht auch du,
oder man hasst dich – hasse du nicht wider,
und sprich auch nicht zu vorlaut oder zu weise;
wenn du träumen kannst, ohne dass die Träume dich beherrschen;
wenn du frei denken kannst, ohne dass Gedanken dein Ziel sind,
wenn du Triumph und Schande beide würdig tragen kannst
und auf beider Wirkung nicht viel gibst;
Wenn du's ertragen kannst, dass die Wahrheit, die du gesagt hast, von Schurken
verdreht wird, um Narren hereinzulegen,
oder alles, wofür du gelebt hast, zerbrochen siehst
und du dann herabsinkst und alles wieder aufbaust mit bereits abgenutztem Werkzeug;
Wenn du all dein Hab und Gut auf einen Haufen wirfst
und auf eine Karte setzt, und es dann verlierst;
und wieder ganz von vorn anfängst
und kein Wort über deinen Verlust verlierst,
Wenn du dein Herz, deine Nerven und all deine Kräfte zusammennehmen kannst,
damit sie dir dienen, obwohl du ausgebrannt bist,
und du so aushältst, obwohl nichts mehr in dir ist
außer der Wille, der ihnen befiehlt: „Haltet durch!“
Wenn du mit Pöbel sprichst und Tugend wahrst,
neben Königen gehst und dabei doch einfach bleibst,
wenn weder geliebter Freund noch erbitterter Feind dir schaden können;
wenn alle dich als Freund betrachten, aber keiner zu sehr,
wenn du die schnell vergängliche Minute
sechzig Sekunden lang mit Sinn füllst,
dann ist dir die Welt Lohn und alles was darin ist,
und – was viel bedeutender ist – du bist ein Mann, mein Sohn!

The *pukka sahib code*
(according to the Ten Commandments and Rudyard Kipling's poem „If …“)

A good white representative of the British Empire has to be a role-model for the natives by

- paying respect to the Ten Commandments
- always maintaining self-control and prestige
- having a high self-esteem that protects one from being influenced by criticism, doubt or hatred and helps one to keep one's head clear in stressful situations
- keeping emotions in balance or being emotionless rather than "touchy"
- being a man of action, a man of honour and strong character who devotes himself to his work

Als Hausarbeit sollen die Schülerinnen und Schüler mithilfe des Hintergrundwissens um den *pukka sahib code* den Rollenkonflikt des Erzählers schriftlich darstellen:

Why is being a "sahib" a problem for the narrator and a reason for his troubled mind?

The narrator wants to fulfil his duty, as he has surely internalised the *pukka sahib code* that demanded of the representatives of the British Empire that they be a model of discipline and superiority in their colonial places. His statement "a white man mustn't be frightened in front of 'natives'" supports this (p. 53, ll. 13–14). Nevertheless, all his instructions and former loyal convictions have gradually deteriorated as a result of his current situation. British rules and codes of conduct are no longer effective in a society that adapts and learns how to evade conflict with its oppressors. The representatives of the system become the victims of their own institutionalised rituals and roles. In this way they put themselves under permanent stress, and if they misbehave or commit an error, they fall prey to the laughter of those they are trying to control. The system has shifted in favour of the oppressed, who undermine it with subtle means to which the rigid, immobile machinery of the Empire and its servants like the subdivisional police officer cannot react. Therefore, the narrator feels that on the one hand he has become a mere puppet of the natives' will. On the other hand, he cannot follow his own will because of his job. So his main problem is that he has already developed an inner distance to his job and government but still cannot act as a free and autonomous individual. Being directed by others like a puppet on a string is what he cannot bear, but is something he has to endure.

1.15 Criticism of colonialism

Zu Beginn der Stunde lesen, korrigieren und ergänzen sich die Schülerinnen ihre Hausarbeiten zum Rollenkonflikt der „sahibs“ gegenseitig. Danach sollen sie miteinander die Textstellen suchen, die ihre Argumentation stützen. Nach ca. 10 Minuten wird eine Schülerin oder ein Schüler beauftragt, die so überarbeitete Hausarbeit vorzutragen und entsprechend auf den Text zu verweisen.

Read out your revised homework and refer to the text.

Folgende Hauptzitate von S. 52, auf die später nochmals zurückgegriffen werden soll, sollen erläutert werden:

a. “And it was at this moment […] that I grasped the hollowness, the futility of the white man’s dominion in the East.” (ll. 11–14)
b. “Here was I, the white man […] – seemingly the leading actor of the piece; but in reality I was only an absurd puppet […].” (ll. 14–17)
c. “I perceived […] that when the white man turns tyrant it is his own freedom that he destroys […]. He becomes a sort of hollow, posing dummy, the conventionalised figure of a sahib.” (ll. 18–21)

Die Reflexion über den Sinn des Kolonialismus und die erklärte Distanz zu dem System seitens des Erzählers lassen eine abstrakte Interpretation der Geschichte zu, wenngleich Orwell selbst seinen Essay eher als „low brow“ bezeichnete. Den Schülerinnen und Schülern kann folgender Impuls für die Transferleistung, derer es bedarf, um den parabelhaften Charakter der Erschießungsszene zu erkennen, gegeben werden:

Orwell’s essay was published in an anti-fascist magazine in 1936, although he had written to the editor:
It all came back to me very vividly the other day and I would like to write it, but it may be that it is quite out of your line. I mean it might be too low brow for your paper and I doubt whether there is anything anti-fascist in the shooting of an elephant.[1]
Do you share Orwell’s doubt or is there something anti-fascist in the shooting of the elephant? Why did the editor publish it after all?

Ideen zur Lösung der Aufgabe werden zunächst im Klassengespräch gesammelt und können an der Tafel als *flow chart* notiert werden:

[1] zitiert nach Sibylle Honeff, George Orwell und der englische Imperialismus, Dissertation Bonn, 1984, S. 149

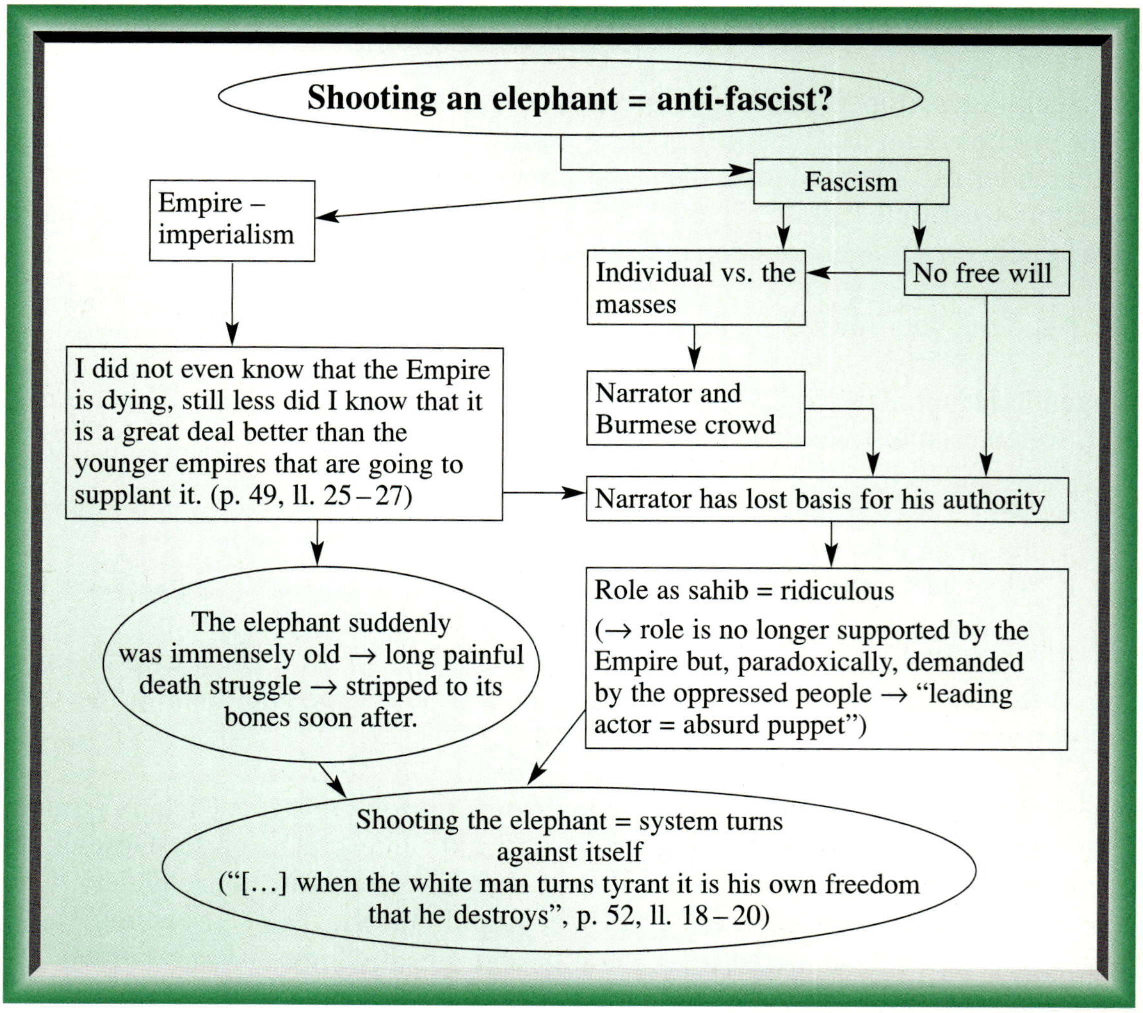

Die schriftliche Ausführung kann als Stillarbeit begonnen und als Hausarbeit fertig gestellt werden.

The shooting was an involuntary act by the police officer, who was forced to carry out the will of the masses that was pressed upon him. In fascist regimes, the individual has to take on a subordinate role and his or her life is directed by the rules and rituals of the masses. But there is an additional symbolical meaning. The narrator says that the imperialist system has become old and rigid. He also describes the elephant as "suddenly stricken, shrunken, immensely old" (p. 53, ll. 39 – 40) so the whole terrible death struggle could be an allusion to the long-term decline of the Empire as a huge but old and rigid system (p. 49, ll. 25 – 27). The coolie who was trampled to death has suffered the fate of all oppressed people: their colonial rulers simply do not care for them and thus treat them inhumanely. In this way, the elephant getting shot by the British officer is a symbol for the dramatic irony of the story: the system of the dominant minority sabotages itself by overestimating its presumed powers and underestimating the intelligence and power of the oppressed masses. The oppressed learn how to outwit their enemies (for example, by giving wrong information, p. 50, ll. 22ff.) and tear down their masquerades of power and thus simply wait for the chance to take revenge and feast on their remains, just as the natives do when they strip the elephant to its bones soon after it has expired.
The story, therefore, is not a simple or "low brow" autobiographical piece of recollection but has the potential to act as a political parable.

Ein Referat oder eine gleichwertig festgestellte Schülerleistung (gfS) kann die Einheit abrunden (Themen s. S. 15).

Doris Lessing, *The Second Hut* (1964)

Die Konzeption des Unterrichtsmodells sieht eine vorbereitende Lektüre vor.

1.16 A struggle to survive

In Partnerarbeit beschäftigen sich die Schülerinnen und Schüler zur Einstimmung mit den ersten beiden Abschnitten der Erzählung (S. 55, Z. 1–26). Sie sollen sich mit der Figur des Major Carruthers vertraut machen und wichtige Aspekte in ein im weiteren Verlauf zu ergänzendes Arbeitsblatt *(Worksheet 12)* eintragen. Im Anschluss daran sollen sie in einem kurzen mündlichen *statement* ihren ersten Eindruck von der Figur des Carruthers formulieren.

Work with your partner. Read the first two paragraphs of the text, underline important information on the main character, Major Carruthers, and fill in the worksheet. Prepare a short oral statement to characterise Carruthers.

Major Carruthers:
- poor
- can't afford the life he and his family want to live
- used to be a soldier
- has always done what was expected of him
- successful soldier
- never liked being a soldier
- soft
- carelessness of dress and carriage
- strained mouth
- gentleman farmer

Carruthers used to be a soldier but was never really happy in his job. He seems to be too soft to be an officer. He always did what his family expected of him. Fulfilling his duty towards his family gave his life its direction and its meaning. When he tries to live his own life, he fails. He is a gentleman farmer but not a very successful one.

Die Ergebnisse der Kurzcharakterisierungen sollten im anschließenden Unterrichtsgespräch gebündelt werden. Besondere Beachtung sollte dabei dem Konzept des „Gentleman Farmers“ geschenkt werden.
In einem nächsten Schritt sollen die Schülerinnen und Schüler in arbeitsteiliger Partnerarbeit Carruthers Familie mit der Van Heerdens vergleichen. Informationen hierzu finden sich in den folgenden Abschnitten (S. 55, Z. 27–S. 57, Z. 4; S. 58, Z. 15–S. 61, Z. 16). Die Ergebnisse werden in Stichworten ebenfalls ins Arbeitsblatt eingetragen.

Scan p. 55, l. 27–p. 57, l. 4 and p. 58, l. 15–p. 61, l. 16 for information on the Carruthers and Van Heerdens families and fill in the rest of the worksheet.

The Carruthers and the Van Heerden families

Fill in information from the text. This worksheet should be completed in the course of your analysis of the story.

	The Carruthers	The Van Heerdens
husband		
wife		
children		
housing		

	The Carruthers	**The Van Heerdens**
husband	– poor – can't afford the life he and his family want to live – used to be a soldier – has always done what was expected of him – successful soldier – never liked to be a soldier – soft – carelessness of dress and carriage – strained mouth – gentleman farmer	– Afrikander – honest, straightforward face – poor – out of work for a long time – uneducated – not used to speaking English
wife	– ill: heart problems – broken down because of their living conditions – stays in bed facing the wall – doesn't complain – accepts defeat – afraid of poverty – used to be pleasant and pretty – perfect wife for a soldier	– vast, slatternly – like a sow among her litter – suspicious – pale eyes – doesn't speak English
children	– two boys – pale – fine-drawn – almost transparent-looking – thin, nervous fairness – defensive and wary – brought up to expect a better life – feel pity for their father – polite, careful, scrupulous – move about the farm like ghosts – attend a boarding school	– nine children – pale, fair-haired
housing	– brave but worn appearance – four-roomed shack – red roof fading to brown – like the house of an apprentice farmer – like a house built as a temporary shelter – good but battered furniture – worn carpets – piano out of tune – untidy	– thatched hut – used to be a store house and a smoke house – well-built – in uncleared bush – round, built of poles and mud, stamped dung floor – one window – full of vermin

An dieser Stelle sollte auf die besondere Situation der Mrs Carruthers aufmerksam gemacht werden. Sie ist als Mitglied der britischen Mittelklasse und als Frau doppelt ausgeschlossen aus der harten Männerwelt der afrikanischen Kolonien. Während Carruthers zumindest zeitweilig Erfüllung in seiner Arbeit findet, flieht sie sich in eine unerklärliche Krankheit, die sich erst ganz am Ende zu bessern scheint, wenn deutlich wird, dass sie ihr Leben nicht länger in einem Land fristen muss, das ihr nie die Chance gab, heimisch zu werden. Als Hausaufgabe soll der Vergleich der Familien schriftlich formuliert werden:

Write a comparison between the two families.

The Carruthers family comes from England. Carruthers used to be quite a successful soldier but was never really happy in this job. For this reason, he decided to go to Africa to become a farmer. Here, he is less successful and his family is on the brink of poverty. This situation causes Carruthers a lot of suffering. He feels guilty because he cannot provide his family with the things they were brought up to expect from life. His wife cannot cope with the situation anymore and finds her escape in a mysterious illness. She wants Carruthers to write to his family for help, but up till this point, he has not been ready to give in.
Van Heerden and his wife are of Dutch origin. They belong to a completely different social class. Van Heerden hasn't had a job for a long time and so he and his large family are terribly poor. They live in a small hut which Carruthers originally thought too primitive for even one man. Van Heerden didn't tell Carruthers about his family because he was afraid that he might not get the job if Carruthers knew that he had a wife and nine children.

1.17 Carruthers and Van Heerden

Nach dem Vorlesen einiger Hausaufgaben sollen, ausgehend von den hier erstellten Texten, die Zukunftsängste des Major Carruthers, die im Schicksal der Familie Van Heerdens konkrete Gestalt angenommen haben, thematisiert werden. Zu diesem Zweck lesen die Schülerinnen und Schüler den hierfür zentralen Abschnitt (S. 61, Z. 17–22). Zur besonderen Hervorhebung bietet sich hier lautes Lesen an.
Im anschließenden Gespräch sollte deutlich werden, dass Carruthers sich davor fürchtet, so arm zu werden wie Van Heerden und seine eigene Familie dem Schicksal der Familie seines Arbeiters auszusetzen.

Read p. 61, l. 17–p. 63, l. 24. What are the fears that Carruthers has and what are his options to improve his situation?

Carruthers sieht drei Lösungsmöglichkeiten:
- er könnte sein Versagen eingestehen und seinen Bruder um Hilfe bitten
- er könnte Van Heerden entlassen, um dessen Elend nicht mehr länger mit ansehen zu müssen, würde damit aber seine Pflicht als Arbeitgeber verletzen
- er könnte die Lebensumstände Van Heerdens verbessern und eine zweite Hütte bauen.

Aufgrund seines Selbstverständnisses als „Gentleman Farmer“, der die Verantwortung für die ihm anvertrauten Arbeitskräfte und ihre Familien trägt, entscheidet Carruthers sich für letzteres.
Die Ergebnisse werden in einem Tafelbild festgehalten.

Carruthers and Van Heerden

Van Heerden's poverty

⇩

Carruthers's worst nightmares

– grim poverty
– children without future

⇩

ways out

⇩	⇩	⇩
turning to his brother	dismissing Van Heerden	building a second hut
⇩	⇩	⇩
admission of defeat	neglect of duty	execution of responsibility
⇩	⇩	⇩
ungentlemanly behaviour	ungentlemanly behaviour	gentlemanly behaviour

Als Vorbereitung auf die nächste Stunde wird folgende kreative Hausaufgabe gestellt:

Carruthers decides to build a second hut for Van Heerden and his family. Read this passage again and write Carruthers's diary on the evening before building begins. Concentrate especially on his problems and fears.

Building will begin tomorrow. Van Heerden is in desperate need of a second hut. I can't imagine how he and his family have managed to live in that small and squalid place so far. What future can he expect for his children? They should go to school, get a decent upbringing. Yes, I'm doing the right thing. It must be done, even if this is very hard on my workers. They haven't had a free weekend for weeks and they need to rest and to recover their strength and their good spirits. But that will have to wait. If they work hard, they can finish it in one day. So it's only one more Sunday that they have to work. But still – I'm worried. Somehow I feel that something will go wrong. Van Heerden cannot deal with natives. He treats them like savages. He doesn't respect them. The bossboy's behaviour was very strange when I told him about the hut. He is usually so cooperative. We both know that we understand each other quite well. But this time it was as if he just switched off when I told him my plans. He went away without saying anything, and I knew he resented my plans. I need him. In fact, he is vitally important. If he says something is alright, the others will follow. But what if he doesn't? I have this strange feeling that something terrible is going to happen.

1.18 The building of the hut

Der Vergleich der Hausaufgabe soll noch einmal auf Carruthers' charakterliche Verfassung hinweisen. Er ist kein Organisator und ein Unterfangen wie das geplante, stellt für ihn ein fast unüberwindliches Hindernis dar.
In Gruppenarbeit sollen die Schülerinnen und Schüler im Anschluss daran die einzelnen Phasen des Hüttenbaus und das Verhalten der beteiligten Parteien erarbeiten und die Ergebnisse in eine Tabelle eintragen *(Worksheet 13)*.

Work in groups of three. Concentrate on the passages about the preparations for the building of the hut and the actual building of it (p. 65, l. 29 – p. 70, l. 14). Fill in the first column (stages of building the hut) together, then work individually and find out how Carruthers, Van Heerden and the natives behave during the different stages.
Fill in the worksheet together.

Mögliche Lösung: s. *Solution sheet 14*.

In einem nächsten Schritt überlegen sich die Gruppen, weshalb der Bau der Hütte unter einem so schlechten Stern stand und an welcher Stelle die beteiligten Gruppen jeweils versagt haben. Die Ergebnisse werden in einem Tafelbild festgehalten.

Discuss in your groups why the building of the hut caused so many problems and at which points Carruthers, Van Heerden or the natives failed.

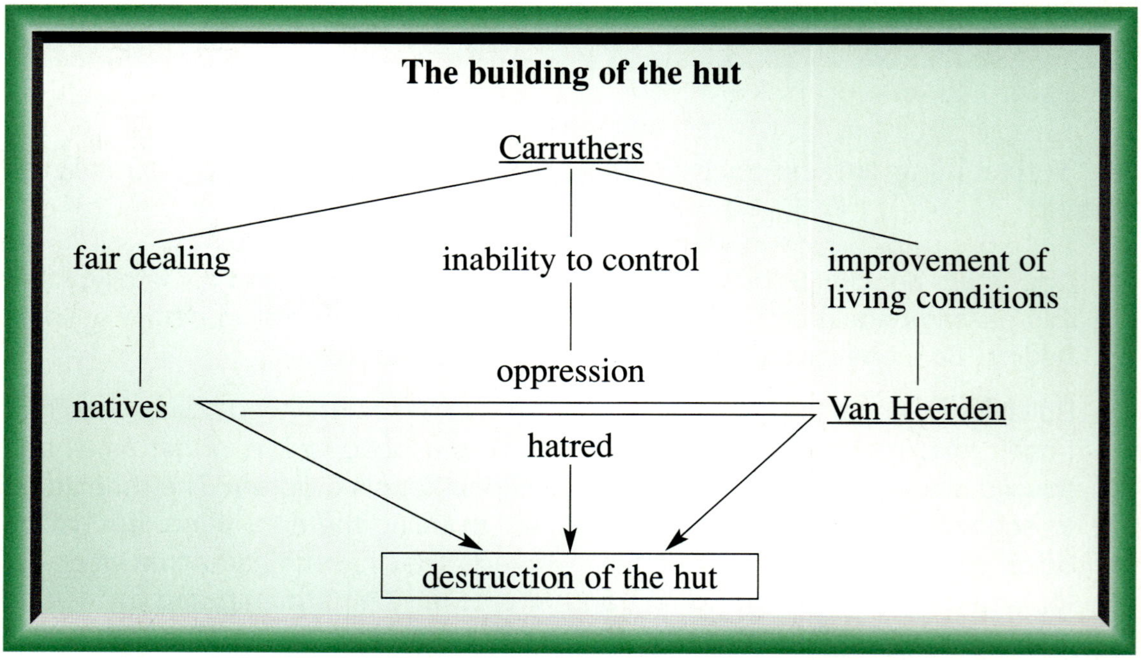

1.19 Defeat

Im Zentrum dieser Stunde steht die Frage, wie die beiden Männer mit dem Tod von Van Heerdens jüngstem Kind umgehen und inwiefern das Erlebnis dieses Todes für Carruthers' Entscheidung, Afrika zu verlassen, verantwortlich ist.

Have another look at p. 71, l. 18 – p. 72, l. 3 and p. 73, l. 10 – p. 74, l. 28. How does Carruthers react to the little girl's death? How does Van Heerden react?

Worksheet 13

Stages of building the hut

Work in groups. Determine the stages of building together but work on Carruthers, Van Heerden and the natives individually. Finally compile your results and discuss them.

	Stages of Building	Carruthers	Van Heerden	Natives	
preparations					behaviour
building					

	Stages of Building	Carruthers	Van Heerden	Natives	
preparations	– the workers are told they will have to work extra hours	– waits for the right moment to tell the natives about his plans – does not show any sympathy for them – tries to be confident that everything will be alright – afraid that something terrible might happen	– happy about the new hut	– the bossboy is unhelpful and hostile – he refuses to accept responsibility – he is not cooperative – the workers show "fierce antagonism"	behaviour
	– the place for the hut is determined – building materials are brought to the site	– determines the place for the hut	– determines the place for the hut		
building		– has to wait for two hours until the others arrive – is angry with the natives but doesn't show his anger – knows the situation is difficult	– is late	– are late – avoid eye contact with Carruthers	
	– a trench for the wall poles is dug	– watches the workers	– is angry because he feels he should have the responsibility for the building of his own hut	– not very enthusiastic	
	– the trench is made deeper	– tells them laughingly to make the trench deeper		– provocative, sulking = beleidigt – make the trench deeper	
	– the poles are put up and bound together				
		– goes home to rest – wakes up later than planned			
			– shouting at the natives – beats one of the natives	– refuse to obey his orders – about to leave	
		– tells the natives to get back to work		– resume work	
		– tells Van Heerden to leave things to him	– angry		
	– the walls are plastered – the hut is finished the following Sunday				

Im Klassengespräch sollte deutlich werden, dass Carruthers versucht, die Würde des Säuglings als menschliches Wesen zu wahren, in dem er alles tut, ihm zu helfen, bzw. als dies zu spät ist, ihm ein christliches Begräbnis zuteil werden zu lassen. Van Heerden hingegen sieht nur ein Kind von vielen. Wenn ein Kind stirbt, wird ein anderes geboren, der Mensch scheint für ihn seine Individualität verloren zu haben und austauschbar geworden zu sein. Carruthers beschließt, Afrika zu verlassen, da er Angst davor hat, genauso abzustumpfen wie Van Heerden. Dies wird besonders in Carruthers' Vision vom „grauen Land der Armut“ deutlich, auf die in diesem Zusammenhang verwiesen werden kann (S. 61, Z. 17–22). Die Ergebnisse werden in einem Tafelbild gebündelt.

Carruthers		**Van Heerden**
respect for the child's dignity as a human being		no respect for the child's dignity: one child is as good as another
⇩		⇩
scared of poverty and its consequences	⇦	if one is poor one cannot afford "fine feelings and scruples and regrets" (p. 73, l. 48)
⇩		⇩
decides to leave the country		struggles on

Eine Kreativaufgabe schließt die Erarbeitung ab. Die Schülerinnen und Schüler sollen noch einmal Carruthers' Situation aufarbeiten und seine Entscheidungen erläutern.

C

Imagine you are Carruthers. Back in England you explain your decision to go home and the factors that led to it in a letter to a good friend.

Dear Ally,
I'm sorry I haven't written sooner. The first months after our return to England have been very busy. We had to find a suitable house and a school for the boys. Both myself and Elizabeth were very exhausted from the long voyage and the troubles of selling the farm and everything else. Leaving Africa was not an easy thing to do – at least not for me. Elizabeth had been longing to go home for many months. It was a relief to her, and her health is improving rapidly. She seems to be a new person, or rather, the person she used to be before we went to the colonies. The boys have settled down well in their new school, and it is a relief to me to see my family happy again and not to feel responsible for their misery.
For me, however, things are not so easy. I loved my farm, although it was a shabby, miserable place, but is was my own. On our farm in Africa, I felt for the first time in my life that I had done something on my own – without the help of my family. Alas, it was not to be. I struggled on as long as I could, much longer than I should have, for my family suffered as a result of my stupid pride. I wanted to make it on my own. I wanted to show – myself more than anyone else – that I could achieve something. But then something happened that made me change my mind, that showed me my true situation and the danger I and my family were in. I needed help on the farm and so I took on an employee. This man was terribly poor and he had a large family: nine children and a pregnant

wife. He was like my worst nightmare come true. When one of his children died in a tragic accident, he wasn't able to mourn for it. Life had been so cruel to him that he didn't have any emotions left. It seemed that he had suffered so much, he could not suffer anymore. He had lost his human dignity. I didn't want to end up like him. This is why I went back home, even though it meant leaving all my dreams behind. Nevertheless, I am responsible for my family. Sometimes one has to abandon one's pride for the sake of those one loves. At times, my thoughts go out to this other family somewhere in the wilderness, and I can only hope they will be treated better by life in future.

Notizen:

Component 2: Cross-Cultural Experiences

R. K. Narayan, *A Horse und Two Goats* (1965)

2.1 Elements of communication

Zur Einstimmung auf die Frage nach dem Wesen funktionierender Kommunikation werden den Schülerinnen und Schülern Themenkärtchen ausgeteilt. Sie erhalten dabei den Auftrag, sich mit ihrem Partner in einem bestimmten Zeitrahmen über dieses Thema zu unterhalten. Da es hier nicht um Inhalte, sondern um das Wesen von Kommunikation geht, sollten die Gesprächsgegenstände so gewählt sein, dass sich auch schwache Schülerinnen und Schüler dazu in der Fremdsprache äußern können. Es empfehlen sich hier also Themen, die sich aus dem Schüleralltag ergeben, z. B. „last weekend", „our next test", „summer holidays", „places to go", etc. (Eine weniger zeitaufwändige Variante dieses Verfahrens ist es, lediglich ein Thema vorzugeben, über das sich die einzelnen Paare individuell unterhalten.) Im Anschluss daran sollen die beiden Partner den Ablauf ihrer Unterhaltung analysieren und eine kurze Definition von „communication" niederschreiben.

Talk with your partner about the subject on the little card I've just given to you. I will tell you when to stop. Then I want you to analyse your conversation and write down a definition of what "communication" is.

Communication takes place between at least two people. Person A says something and person B listens and reacts verbally. Then person A listens in turn and reacts to what person B has said and so on. Communication is interactive. It can only work if the partners understand each other.

Nach dem Vorlesen einzelner Schülerarbeiten wird das Ergebnis der Fragestellung an der Tafel festgehalten:

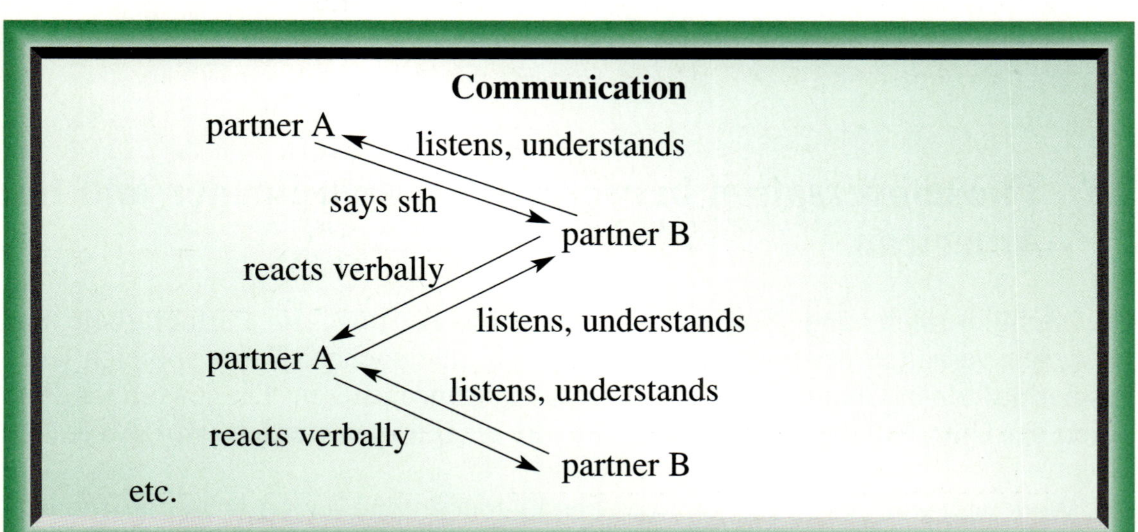

Im Anschluss daran wird die *short story* entweder als Ganzes oder zumindest bis zu S. 76, Z. 34 über CD präsentiert. Die Schülerinnen und Schüler erhalten dabei den Auftrag, sich beim Zuhören besonders auf die Unterhaltung zwischen dem amerikanischen Touristen und dem indischen Bauern zu konzentrieren.

Listen to the CD. Concentrate on the conversation between the American tourist and the Indian farmer.

Im Unterrichtsgespräch wird nun geklärt, was das Besondere an der Unterhaltung der beiden Charaktere ist und weshalb sie nicht funktioniert. Dabei kann das vorher erstellte Tafelbild entsprechend modifiziert werden. Gerade das Nicht-Verstehen des Gegenübers beim gleichzeitigen Beharren beider Partner auf dem Fortführen der Konversation macht die Komik der vorgeführten Situation aus.

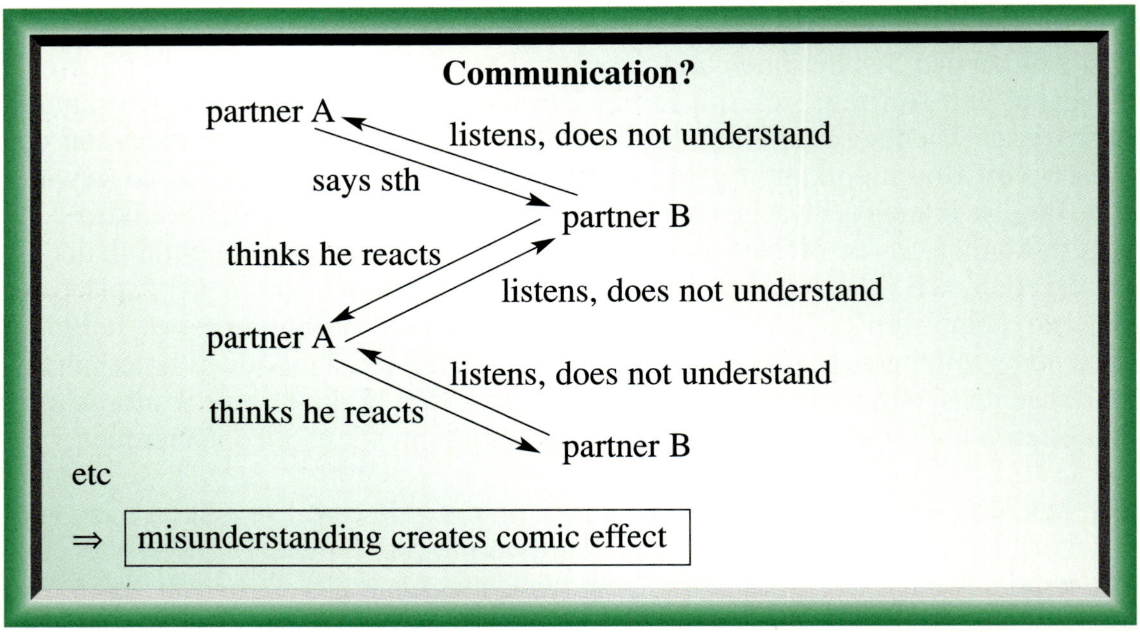

Als Hausaufgabe werden folgende vorbereitende Aufträge erteilt:

1. Read and prepare the complete story.
2. Concentrate on the conversation between the American and the Indian. Underline their parts in the conversation in different colours.

2.2 The conversation between the Indian farmer and the American

Die Schülerinnen und Schüler erhalten den Auftrag, in Partnerarbeit das Gesprächsverhalten der beiden Redepartner zu untersuchen. Dabei soll sich jeder Partner auf einen Charakter aus der Erzählung konzentrieren. Die jeweiligen Passagen der Unterhaltung sollen in eine Tabelle eingetragen werden *(Worksheet 15)*.

Work with your partner. One of you has to concentrate on the American, the other on the Indian. Fill in the worksheet.

Worksheet 15

The Indian farmer and the American tourist: A conversation?

Work with your partner.
Partner A: Concentrate on the Indian farmer
Partner B: Concentrate on the American tourist.
Fill in the respective passages of their conversation.

The Indian farmer	**The American tourist**
	How do you do?
My name is Muni and the goats are mine, no matter what other people will tell you.	
	Do you smoke?
I don't know anything about the murder.	

Lösungen zu Worksheet 15:

The Indian farmer	The American tourist
	How do you do?
My name is Muni and the goats are mine, no matter what other people will tell you.	
	Do you smoke?
I don't know anything about the murder.	
	I come from America – do you know America?
The times are bad. It's the fault of the cinema.	
	Do you know when this horse was made?
Please leave me alone. There are no bad people in our village.	
	I have come from far away to see your beautiful country, the country of my dreams.
Sometimes our cattle are lost but our astrologer can help us.	
	Is this your statue? Will you sell it to me?
The statue is very old.	
	I really do want this statue.
This horse will appear as the tenth avatar at the end of the Yuga.	
	I will pay any reasonable price.
God Vishnu has come nine times before.	
	I am not a millionaire.
The first avatar was in the shape of a fish.	
	Transportation will be my problem.
God Vishnu alone saves mankind.	
	I can take the horse in my car.
I hope you have a lot of children.	
	Will you take a hundred rupees for it?
Our village headman can change the money for you.	
	I could go a little higher.
He doesn't like me, that's why I never let my goats go near his farm.	

Sind die Arbeitsblätter ausgefüllt, werden sie in der Mitte zertrennt. Jeder Schüler erhält so die Redeanteile „seines“ Charakters. In einem zweiten Arbeitsschritt sollen nun diese Fragmente zu einer funktionierenden Konversation erweitert werden.

Cut your worksheets in two halves and fill in the missing parts so that you get a "real" conversation.

Im Folgenden werden nur die den oben aufgelisteten Antworten entsprechenden Fragen aufgeführt.

The Indian farmer
- What is your name and how do other people see you?
- Do you know anything about the murder that happened in the area?
- How would you describe the times in which you live? Who is responsible for the current situation?
- Can you tell me anything about any bad characters in your village?
- Are there any dangers for your cattle and who can you turn to for help?
- Can you tell me anything about the age of the statue?
- What will the horse appear as in the end and when will this be?
- How often has Vishnu come before?
- Who saves mankind?
- What do you think of my family?
- Who can change my money?
- How would you describe your relationship to the village headman?

Die Schülerarbeiten sollen in der Hausaufgabe verwendet werden, um die Personen zu charakterisieren:

Use the conversation you have invented to write a characterisation of your person.

Muni, the Indian Farmer
Muni was born in a small village somewhere in India. He comes from a poor family and he has never gone to school or had the chance to train for a job. He has never owned much money and he has never seen banknotes of a high value. In the village, he is not regarded very highly because he belongs to its poorest members. Muni is afraid of the authorities because he knows that people like him haven't got the slightest chance if they get into trouble. His two goats are everything he owns; they guarantee his survival. Accordingly, it is a terrible thing for him if they get lost in the fields. Muni then turns to the village astrologer for help. He is a very pious person and he expects his salvation to come from Vishnu.

2.3 Materialistic and idealistic values

Die in den beiden vorangegangenen Stunden analysierte Unterhaltung dreht sich in all ihren Missverständnissen und komischen Wendungen um zwei wesentliche Bereiche der menschlichen Gesellschaft, um Geld und Religion. Während der Amerikaner mit der typischen Selbstverständlichkeit des westlichen Touristen in einem Entwicklungsland der Meinung ist, mit Geld ließe sich alles kaufen, bestimmen Heil und Erlösung, repräsentiert durch die vor seinem Dorf aufgestellte Götterstatue, das Leben des Inders. Ironischerweise ist am Ende er es, der durch den vermeintlichen Geschäftssinn des Amerikaners profitiert, während der ausländische Tourist mit leeren Händen ausgeht.

Die Schülerinnen und Schüler sollen in Gruppenarbeit das in dieser *short story* aufgezeigte Verhältnis von materiellen und ideellen Werten untersuchen und ihre Ergebnisse anhand einer Grafik präsentieren.
Jede Gruppe erhält hierfür eine Folie und entsprechende Stifte und präsentiert im Anschluss an die Gruppenarbeit ihr Ergebnis vor dem Plenum. Zur Ergebnissicherung können die einzelnen Grafiken für die gesamte Klasse kopiert werden.

Work in groups of four. Analyse the relationship between materialistic and idealistic values represented by the money of the American tourist and the statue in the Indian village. Present the results of your analysis in a graph.

Mögliche Lösung:

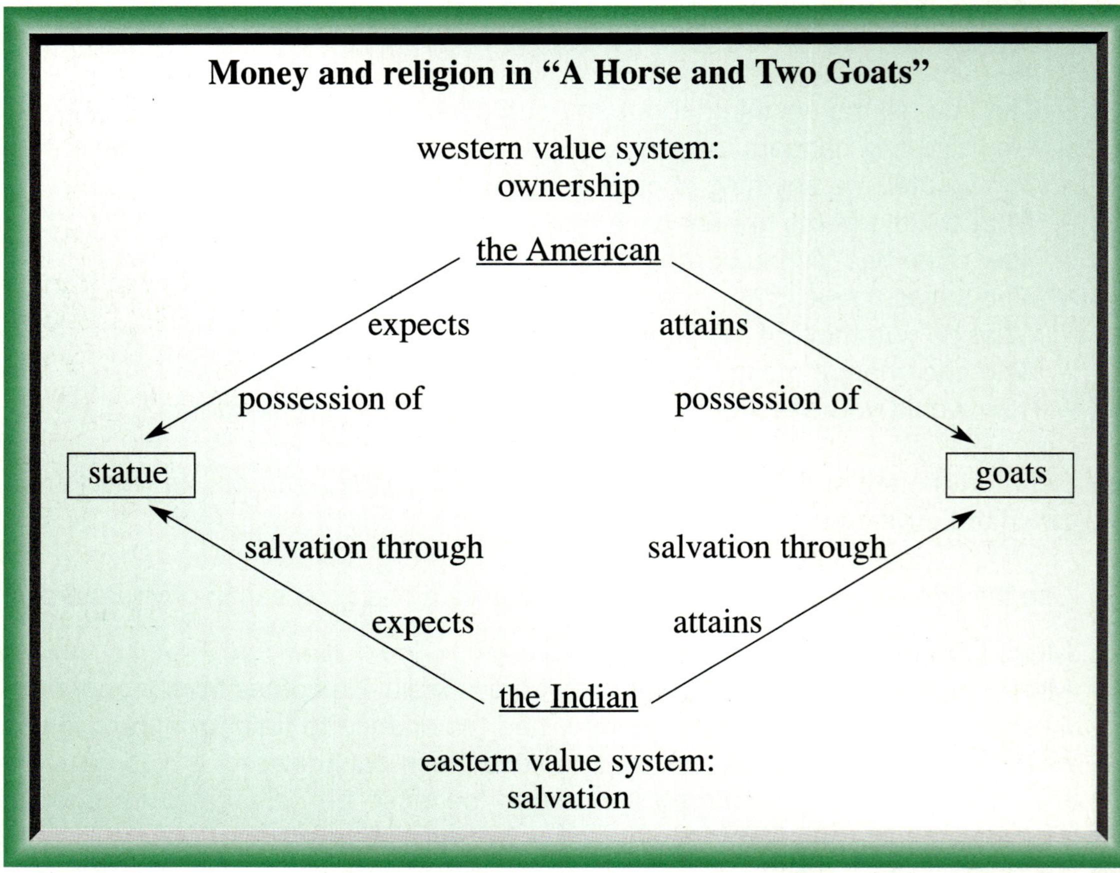

Notizen:

Chinua Achebe, *Dead Men's Path* (1972)

Vorbemerkung zum Einsatz der CD:

Der Text auf CD wird von einem afrikanischen Leser vorgetragen. Sein Idiom ist authentisch und daher für Lernende gelegentlich ungewohnt. Es ist zu empfehlen, die Aufnahme nicht am Anfang zum reinen Hörverstehen einzusetzen, es sei denn man möchte die Sprache des Sprechers thematisieren. Besser ist es, wenn die Schülerinnen und Schüler den Text mitlesen. Wenn genügend Zeit zur Verfügung steht, lohnt es sich, die Aufnahme nach der Textbesprechung einzuspielen. So wird zum einen der Inhalt noch einmal wiederholt. Zum anderen kann Bezug zum Leitthema: *One Language – Many Voices* bzw. *Echoes of the Empire* genommen werden. Hieran könnte sich ein Schülervortrag zum Thema *Varieties of English in Africa* oder zum Thema „Englisch als Amtssprache" (*English as official language in the colonies*) anschließen.

2.4 Tradition and progress

Die Schülerinnen und Schüler sollen sich zunächst mit den positiven und negativen Aspekten von Fortschritt beschäftigen. Zu diesem Zweck erhält jeder Schüler drei grüne und drei rote Karten, auf denen er Vorteile (grün) und Nachteile (rot) von Fortschritt festhält. Pro Karte darf nur ein Stichwort notiert werden. Die Karten werden eingesammelt und farblich geordnet auf einer Pinwand angebracht. Ist im Klassenzimmer keine Pinwand vorhanden bzw. kann keine zusätzlich aufgestellt werden, so kann man die Karten auch mit Klebestreifen auf einem großen Bogen Packpapier anbringen, den man im Klassenzimmer aufhängt.

Write down three positive and three negative aspects of "progress": use the green cards for positive aspects and the red ones for negative aspects. We will collect the cards on the pinboard.

positive aspects:
- innovation
- improvement
- better living conditions
- life becomes easier
- diseases can be cured
- dangerous or hard jobs can be done by machines

negative aspects:
- loss of traditions
- important knowledge will be lost
- machines become more important than people
- loss of jobs
- neglect of the environment
- pollution

Die Schülerinnen und Schüler sollen nun aus den drei für sie wichtigsten positiven und negativen Aspekten unter Benutzung eines Stichwortzettels einen kurzen mündlichen Vortrag zum Thema *The positive and negative aspects of progress* vorbereiten.

Have a close look at all the cards, then choose those three positive and three negative aspects that you consider most important – they need not necessarily be your own – and prepare a short speech on the positive and negative sides of progress. You can use notes but you must not write down a complete text and then read it out to your audience.

Ladies and gentlemen,
In the following talk, I would like to consider some positive and negative aspects of progress. The term "progress" is usually connected with positive aspects like the improvement of working conditions, medical care, or living standards in general. Certainly, if we compare our lives to the lives of people in the Middle Ages, we can definitely say that progress in so many fields has made our lives much easier and securer.
As little as one hundred years ago, things that are quite simple for us today meant hardship and toil. If we want to have a bath, for example, we just turn on the tap. A hundred years ago, many people had to go to the local well to get water, cut wood to make a fire, heat the water, pour it into a tub and then empty it from the tub again with a scoop. – A very simple example, but it shows us the blessings of progress very explicitly.
But is progress only a good thing? Let us go back to the Middle Ages. People lived hard lives, certainly, but they lived in an unspoilt environment. Rivers were not polluted, the air was clear and the climate more constant. We pay a high price for our luxurious lives. Many parts of the eco-system have been destroyed and cannot be repaired again. This will be felt more acutely by the generations to come. But there are other negative aspects of progress which relate to us more immediately. Progress also brings advanced technology and this means an increasing redundancy of jobs because many things that, in the past, were done by people are now done by machines.
To conclude, progress is not an absolute value, it must be seen in perspective. It is only a good thing if it is used sensibly and for the good of people.

Nach dem Vortrag einiger Reden folgt die eigentliche Textarbeit. Die Schülerinnen und Schüler konzentrieren sich zunächst auf die Zukunftsvorstellungen des jungen Lehrerehepaares Mike und Nancy. Dabei sollte besonders auf Mike Obis Rolle als „pivotal teacher“ (S. 80, Z. 9) hingewiesen werden, aufgrund deren gerade er in der Lage sein sollte, beide Seiten zu sehen, die des Fortschritt bringenden Kolonialismus und die der Hergebrachtes bewahrenden Stammestradition. Die Ergebnisse werden an der Tafel festgehalten.

Read p. 80 ll. 1–24. Underline the things we learn about Mike and Nancy.

Plans for the future

Mike	Nancy
– wonderful ideas	– beautiful gardens
– against narrow views	– everything: modern and delightful
– modern methods	
⇓	⇓
a high standard of teaching	a beautiful school compound

Mike's and Nancy's plans are literally crossed by the natives' "dead men's path". Read on up to p. 82, l. 11. Collect information on the importance of the path.

Das bereits erstellte Tafelbild wird um die Informationen über den Weg der Eingeborenen erweitert.

Plans for the future

<u>Mike</u>
- wonderful ideas
- against narrow views
- modern methods

⇓

a high standard of teaching

dead men's path

<u>Nancy</u>
- beautifiul gardens
- everything: modern and delightful

⇓

a beautiful school compound

- connects the village shrine with the place of burial
- has always been there
- dead relatives depart by it
- ancestors use it to visit the village
- children arrive via it when they are born

Die Hausaufgabe konzentriert sich auf Michael Obi:

1. Read and prepare the complete story.
2. How does Michael Obi deal with the situation in his conversations with his colleague and with the village chief? Underline his actions and the reasons for them in two different colours.

2.5 Intolerance

Die Ergebnisse der Hausaufgabe werden in einem Tafelbild gesichert.

Michael Obi's actions	**Michael Obi's reasons**
– he forbids the villagers to use the path	– the villagers might use the school grounds for pagan rituals during the inspection
– he bars the path with sticks and barbed wire	– the purpose of the school is to eradicate superstition
⇓	⇓
Obi uses undue violence	in his fight against backwardness

Ausgehend von diesem Tafelbild sollen die Schülerinnen und Schüler Obis zunächst durchaus positiv zu wertenden Innovationswillen als kontraproduktiv für seine eigenen Ideale erkennen. Seine Intoleranz gegenüber anderen schafft weitere Intoleranz ihm selbst gegenüber.

Work with your partner. Describe the mechanisms that Obi's "misguided zeal" sets in motion and that bring about the destruction of his work. Present your findings in the form of a graph. Then form groups of six (three teams) and discuss your graphs.

Ein oder zwei Möglichkeiten werden in der Klasse vorgestellt. Dazu haben die Gruppen Folien erhalten.

The Mechanism of intolerance

progress ⟷ **destroys by intolerance** ⟷ tradition

Als kreative Hausaufgabe soll der Bericht des Aufsichtsbeamten geschrieben werden:

You are the supervisor. Write his full report.

Dear Sirs,
On my visit to Ndume Central School, I found myself confronted with a most shocking situation. The school buildings were in a deplorable state. One of them had even been pulled down completely so that it is impossible to use it for further teaching, which leaves the school short of classrooms. The school grounds are in a state of devastation: hedges have been torn up, flowers trampled to the ground and the lawn has been rendered completely useless for ball games and other recreational activities. All in all, the situation in Ndume is not at all favourable to a successful educational process.
Worst of all, however, is the tension between the headmaster and the villagers, which is coming close to a tribal war. Apparently, Mr Obi, in whom we all put so much hope, has been unable to establish peaceful and friendly links with the population of the village. The misguided zeal with which he has tried to realise his dreams of a modern school has only led to intolerance towards the values of others. This in turn has generated new intolerance on the side of the natives. Therefore, I would very much advise the appropriate authorities to replace Mr and Mrs Obi with someone who sees progress not as an end in itself, but as the means to bring about tolerance and understanding and thus create a better future for all the people in Ndume.

Es könnte sich hier das Anhören und Besprechen der CD-Aufnahme anschließen, wie eingangs unter den Vorbemerkungen zum Einsatz der CD erläutert.

Notizen:

Ngugi wa Thiong'o, *A Meeting in the Dark* (1974)

Die Konzeption des Unterrichtsmodells sieht eine vorbereitende Lektüre vor.

2.6 The relationship between parents and son

Im Mittelpunkt dieser Stunde steht das Verhältnis Johns zu seinen Eltern und zu seiner Geliebten. John ist hin- und hergerissen zwischen der durch den Calvinismus seines Vaters repräsentierten Kolonialkultur und der durch Wamuhu und ihre Familie repräsentierten Stammeskultur. Die Schülerinnen und Schüler sollen erkennen, welchem Druck John durch die an Fanatismus grenzende religiöse Überzeugung seines Vaters ausgesetzt ist und wie er schließlich an den an ihn gestellten zu hohen Erwartungen zerbricht.
In Gruppenarbeit sollen die Charakterisierungen der Personen angefertigt werden. Die Aufgabenstellung sollte stichwortartig auf dem Overheadprojektor für die Lerngruppe mit – und während der Erarbeitung nachlesbar sein. Es kann auch ein kleiner *task*-Zettel an alle ausgegeben werden (*Task sheet 16*).

Concentrate on p. 83, l. 1–p. 85, l. 23. Work in groups of three. Each group member has to concentrate on either John, his father or his mother. Scan the text for information on "your" person and his or her relationship to the other two. Then write a short characterisation of your person and read it to the members of your group.
Use the characterisations of your group to design a poster which shows the relationships between John, Stanley and Susanna. Present your poster in class.

John:	**Stanley:**	**Susanna:**
– fears his father – avoids his father – has sth to hide – feels guilty – looks to his mother for help – feels tortured by his father – is "mortally afraid" of his father – feels trapped by his father – hates his father – makes his father responsible for his own problems – hasn't got the courage to rebel against his father	– stopped his wife from telling John stories – sees John as a sinner – thinks John has to be watched – wants John to learn about Jesus – inflicts moral torture on John – probably sees John as simply the result of a sin that he committed – thinks everybody has to be saved – thinks women are morally not as strong as men – calls his wife "sister" – is cruel to John	– obeys her husband – has been married for a long time – had been happy with Stanley before he became a convert – sinned with Stanley before their marriage – thinks of leaving Stanley – does not know what is troubling John – fears for him

Characterisation of John
John is a young man who suffers under a dominant father. His father does not see him as a human being but as an object for his religious zeal. John is terribly afraid of him and hasn't got the power to stand up to him. Because of this, John suffers in silence knowing that nothing will ever change. The situation is made worse by the fact that John has something to hide from his father. As a result of his awareness of the injustice with which he is treated by his father, he makes him responsible for his own situation from which he cannot escape. He feels trapped and despises himself for not having the courage to fight against his father's power over him.

Characterisation of Stanley
Stanley converted to Christianity in his youth and is now an almost fanatic preacher of his new faith. Before his conversion, he was a young man like many others from his tribe. However, his new religion has changed his whole personality. He condemns his former behaviour and partly blames his wife for having had sexual intercourse with her before their marriage. The result of this pre-marital relationship is his son, John. For this reason John, more than anyone else, is the target of Stanley's religious zeal. He educates him in the fear of God and His commandments and perverts the idea of religious obedience into an instrument of personal dominance and moral torture. In his struggle to save everybody from sin, he neglects people's personalities, their backgrounds and their wishes. He calls his wife "sister" and forbids her telling their son the old stories of their tribe. In doing so, he prevents John from knowing his roots and growing up as a stable personality.

Characterisation of Susanna
Susanna has been Stanley's wife for a long time and in their youth, before Stanley's conversion, they were happy. Susanna, too, has converted to Christianity and obeys her husband when he tells her not to talk about the old stories of their tribe although she is not convinced about her husband's radical break with his ethnic background. Susanna does not really know what is troubling John but she fears for him because she clearly sees that he is close to breaking under the strain of having to meet his father's expectations. However, Susanna remains passive and does not do anything to improve the situation.

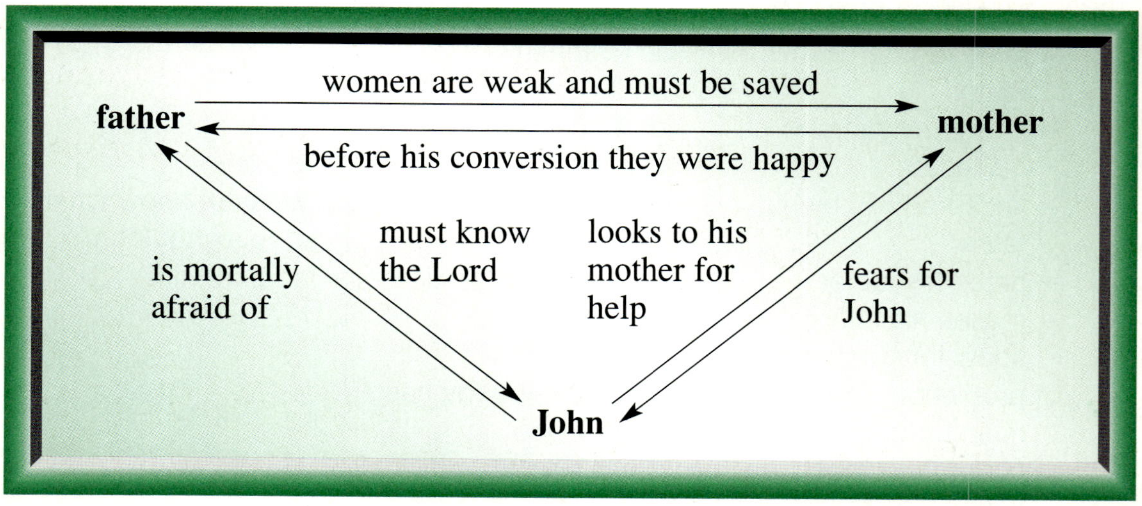

Bei der Präsentation werden die Lernenden an die Regeln eines guten Vortrages erinnert und entsprechend in ihrer Haltung und Rede korrigiert. (Weitere Informationen hierzu sind zu finden in Schallhorn/Peschel, *Method Guide*, Schöningh: Paderborn, 2004)

Tasks for teams: The relationship between parents and son

Your task:

- Concentrate on p. 83, l. 1–p. 85, l. 23.
- Work in groups of three.
- Each group member has to concentrate on either John, his father or his mother.
- Scan the text for information on "your" person and his or her relationship to the other two.
- Write a short characterisation of your person and read it to the members of your group.
- Correct and help each other.
- Speak in English only!

Present!

- Use the characterisations of your group to design a poster which shows the relationships between John, Stanley and Susanna.
- Make sure your writing is big enough to be seen from the back of your classroom.
- Present your poster in class keeping in mind all presentation skills you have learnt so far.

Tasks for teams: The relationship between parents and son

Your task:

- Concentrate on p. 83, l. 1–p. 85, l. 23.
- Work in groups of three.
- Each group member has to concentrate on either John, his father or his mother.
- Scan the text for information on "your" person and his or her relationship to the other two.
- Write a short characterisation of your person and read it to the members of your group.
- Correct and help each other.
- Speak in English only!

Present!

- Use the characterisations of your group to design a poster which shows the relationships between John, Stanley and Susanna.
- Make sure your writing is big enough to be seen from the back of your classroom.
- Present your poster in class keeping in mind all presentation skills you have learnt so far.

In einem anschließenden Unterrichtsgespräch soll Stanleys Vorstellung vom Christentum thematisiert werden. Dabei soll deutlich werden, dass er, in einem völlig missverstandenen religiösen Eifer, die Menschen durch Ausübung von Druck und Verhängung von Strafen zu ihrem Seelenheil zwingen will. Seine wirkliche Aufgabe wäre es, wie dies die christliche Lehre besagt, die Mitglieder seiner Gemeinde dazu zu bringen, ihr Seelenheil aus eigener Überzeugung anzustreben. Folgende Hilfsfragen können zur Orientierung dienen:

- What is ~~John's~~ Stanley's idea of Christian religion?
- How does he define it?
- How does he express his religious convictions in his daily life?
- In which way does he influence others?

Die Ergebnisse der Diskussion werden in einem Tafelbild festgehalten.

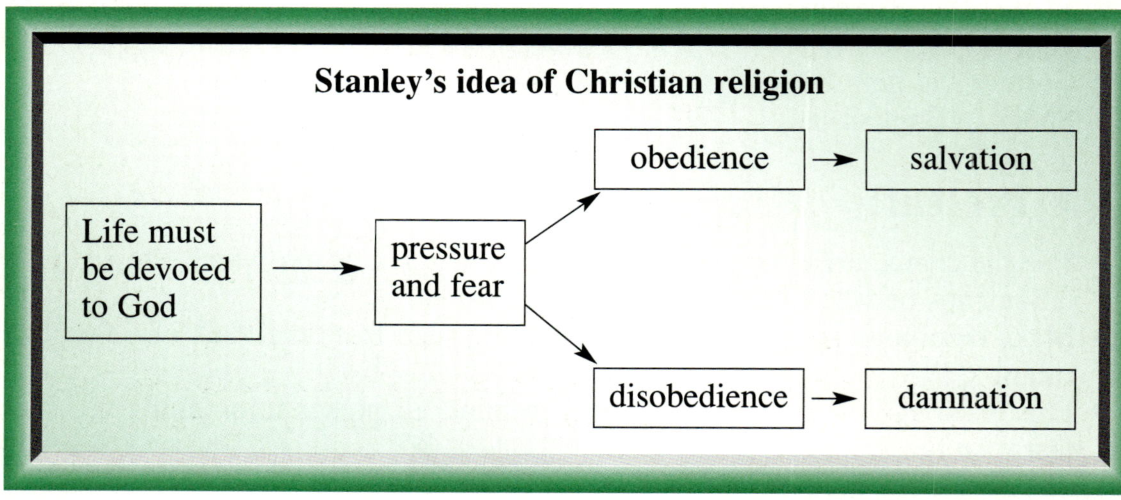

Das Verhältnis zwischen John und Wamuhu soll in schriftlicher Hausarbeit erörtert werden.
Nachdem das Verhältnis Johns zu seinen Eltern und vor allem zu seinem Vater geklärt worden ist, soll in der Folgestunde Johns Verhalten gegenüber Wamuhu mit dem seines Vaters gegenüber seiner Mutter verglichen werden. Zur Vorbereitung dieses Themenkomplexes erarbeiten die Schülerinnen und Schüler in der Hausaufgabe das Verhältnis der beiden jungen Liebenden.

Read the passages which tell us about John and Wamuhu. Describe their relationship in about 200 words.

The relationship between John and Wamuhu
Wamuhu is a girl from the village. She is not educated in the western sense of the word and her family still follows the traditions of the tribe. While her father is reluctant to give his consent to her relationship with John, her mother sees it as a chance for her daughter to rise socially and have a better life in the future.
John knows that in his father's eyes, such a relationship would be wrong and even in this situation, he cannot escape his father's overpowering influence. However, John is not quite sure whether he might really love Wamuhu if his own social position and his private situation were different. Wamuhu is pregnant, but she has not told her parents yet and John wants her to wait until he has left the country. Marriage seems impossible to John because he is afraid of his father and of what other people would say about him. He does not really know his feelings towards Wamuhu, so he decides to offer her money for the child. When Wamuhu declines the offer, he gets enraged and, in the end, kills her. (190 words)

2.7 Comparison of father and son

Nach dem Verlesen und Kommentieren einiger Hausaufgaben sollen die Schülerinnen und Schüler das Verhalten Johns in Bezug auf seine Geliebte mit dem Verhalten seines Vaters in Bezug auf seine Mutter vergleichen. Dabei sollen Parallelen und Unterschiede in den Reaktionen der beiden Männer auf ähnliche Situationen aufgezeigt werden. Die Ergebnisse werden in einem Tafelbild festgehalten.

Compare John's behaviour towards Wamuhu to his father's behaviour towards his mother in this situation.

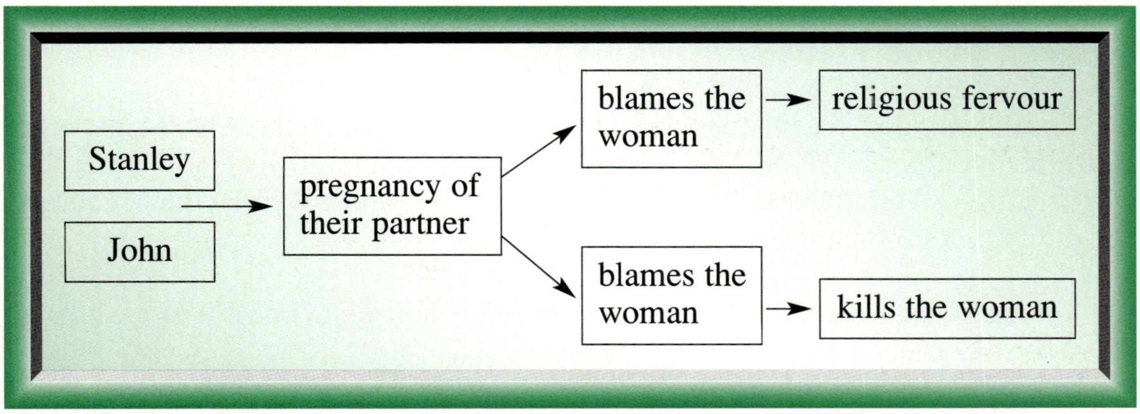

Wamuhus Vater vergleicht im Gespräch mit seiner Frau die traditionelle Lebensweise des Stammes mit der neuen Welt der Weißen, die alte Werte mehr und mehr verdrängt, ohne sie wirklich ersetzen zu können. Dieses Dilemma steht nachfolgend im Mittelpunkt.

Read p. 88, ll. 9–32. What does Wamuhu's father say about the old and the new times? How does he see these changes?

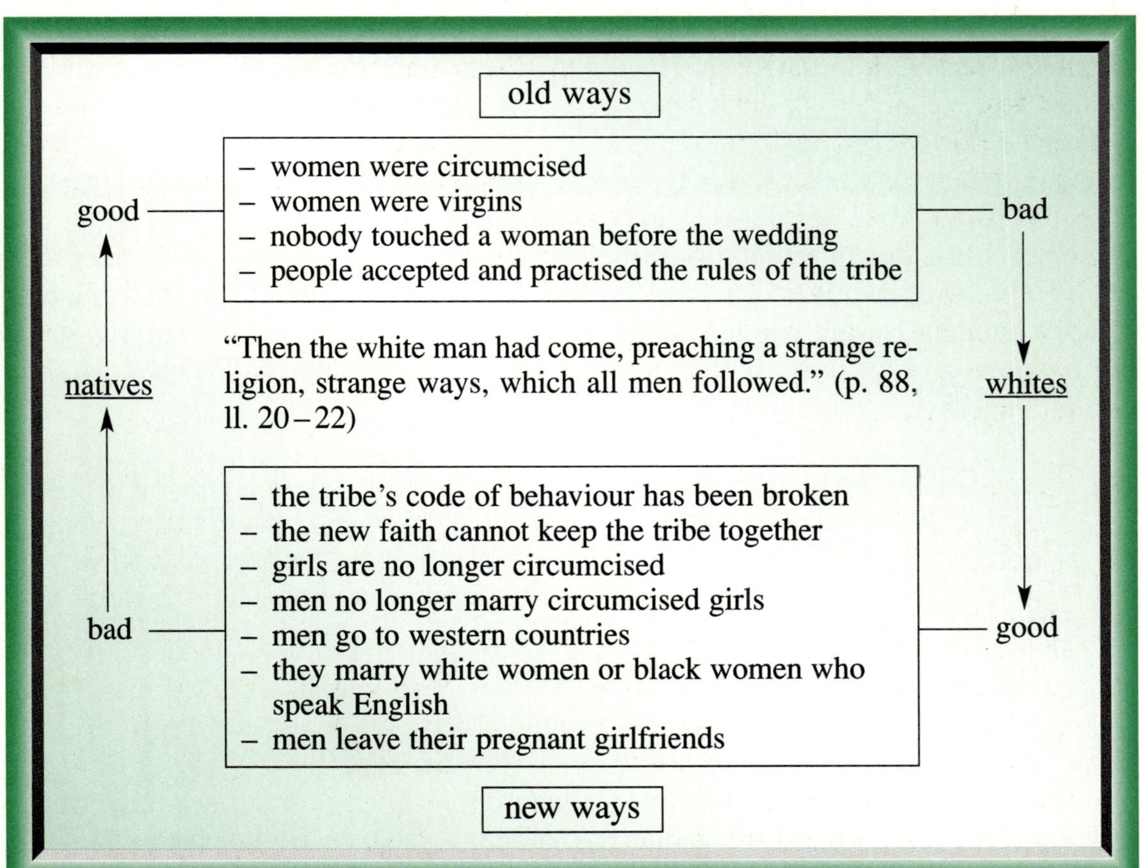

2.8 Cultural clash

Zur Einstimmung auf das Thema der Stunde sollen die Schülerinnen und Schüler sich Gedanken über den Einfluss der Gesellschaft auf den Einzelnen machen. Zur Vorbereitung des Unterrichtsgesprächs schreibt jeder auf bereitgestellte Karten drei Bereiche auf, in denen er sich als von der Gesellschaft beeinflusst sieht (jeweils ein Begriff pro Karte). Die Karten werden nach Kategorien geordnet an eine Pinwand geheftet. (Die Begriffe können auch einfach geordnet an die Tafel geschrieben werden.)

Think about your position in society. Write down three areas where you feel you are influenced by society.

Das anschließende Unterrichtsgespräch sollte der Frage nach der Abhängigkeit des Einzelnen von gesellschaftlichen Normen nachgehen und positive sowie negative Aspekte dieses Verhältnisses aufzeigen. Im Anschluss daran werden die Ergebnisse auf die Figur des John übertragen.

Underline passages in the text that show the influence of society as a whole on John's decisions and actions.

John and society
- people expect John to be polite
- John is not like the other educated young men
- John is loyal to the tribe
- he is a "model of humility and human perfection"
- he feels proud that people should think well of him
- he is afraid of disappointing the villagers
- he is judged by stricter rules than others
- he is torn between conflicting values
- he has no identity

Zum Abschluss der Interpretationsarbeit sollen die Schülerinnen und Schüler sich noch einmal vergegenwärtigen, welche Mechanismen die Charaktere in der Erzählung so handeln lassen, wie sie handeln. Hierfür bietet sich eine Diskussion in einer *fishbowl* an (zur praktischen Durchführung siehe Schallhorn/Peschel: *Method Guide*, Paderborn: Schöningh 2004, S. 69ff.)

Choose either the character of John, Stanley or Susanna. Imagine the following situation: John has been sentenced and is now in prison, where he is given the opportunity to meet his parents and talk to them about his feelings and why he committed the crime. His parents in turn explain their behaviour towards him. Discuss in a fishbowl style.

Component 3: Postcolonial Consequences

Muriel Spark, *The Black Madonna* (1963)

3.1 Family life

Zur Einstimmung auf die *short story* werden Schülerinnen und Schüler dazu aufgefordert, ihre Assoziationen zu der Darstellung der schwarzen Madonna in der Collage auf den *Getting started*-Seiten der Textausgabe still aufzuschreiben. Die Stichwörter werden dann in Partnerarbeit in einer Mind-Map organisiert. Idealerweise werden hier bereits die zentralen Themen der *short story* angesprochen.

Look carefully at the picture and write down all the things which you associate with the statue. This should take you no more than three minutes. After this, work with your partner and organise your keywords in a mindmap.

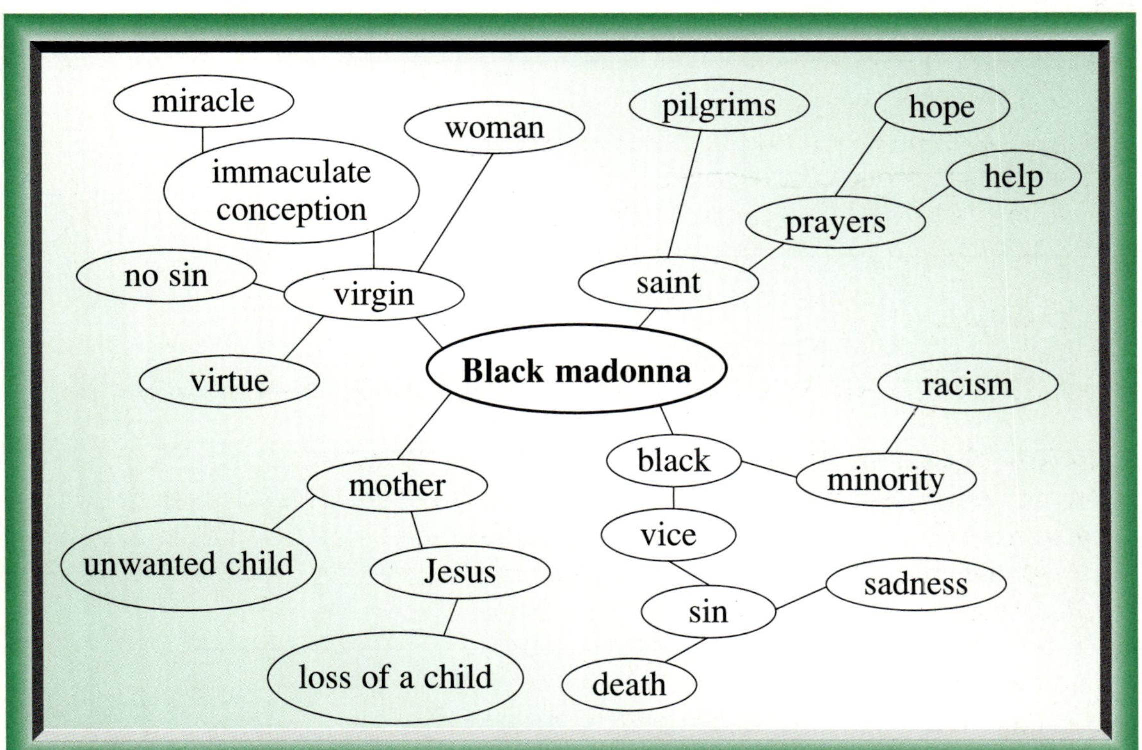

Zunächst beschäftigen sich die Schülerinnen und Schüler mit dem Familienleben und dem Lebensstil der Hauptpersonen Lou und Raymond. Die wichtigsten Aspekte werden dazu in eine Tabelle eingetragen. Die zweite Spalte bleibt der Person der Elizabeth vorbehalten und wird in der zweiten Stunde ergänzt. Die Lerngruppe kann mit dem Arbeitsblatt (*Worksheet 17*) arbeiten.

Work with your partner. Read p. 96, l. 5–p. 98, l. 7. What do we learn about the everyday life of Lou and Raymond? Fill in the grid together.

Worksheet 17

The lives of Lou, Raymond and Elizabeth

Scan the text for information on Lou's, Raymond's and Elizabeth's lives. Fill in the grid.

	Lou and Raymond	Elizabeth
hometown		
house		
flat		
jobs		
married life		
pastimes		
religion		
friends		

Lösungen zu Worksheet 17:

	Lou and Raymond	Elizabeth
hometown	– Whitney Clay	
house	– new council house – block of flats	
flat	– fifth floor – three-roomed flat	
jobs	– Lou: used to be a nurse – Raymond: foreman at the motor works	
married life	– no children – married for quite a while	
pastimes	– reading (magazines, books) – no TV – rarely go to the cinema	
religion	– Catholic – take an active interest in their congregation – members of church committees	
friends	– choose their friends carefully	

Im anschließenden Unterrichtsgespräch wird der Lebensstil der beiden Hauptfiguren als „aspiring middle class" charakterisiert. Anhaltspunkte hierfür sind die Dreizimmerwohnung (das Ehepaar hat keine Kinder, also ist ein Zimmer „übrig"), die Freizeitbeschäftigungen (das Lesen sorgfältig ausgewählter Werke statt Fernsehen), das soziale Engagement und die Wahl der Freunde bzw. Bekannten.
Als Vorbereitung auf die nächste Stunde soll der Text zu Ende gelesen werden. Dabei sollen alle Informationen zum Verhältnis des Paares zu den Jamaikanern, Henry und Oxford, markiert werden:

1. Read and prepare the complete text.
2. Underline passages in the text that tell you about the relationship between Lou and Raymond and the two new characters, Henry and Oxford.

3.2 The Jamaicans and Elizabeth's lot

Die Ergebnisse der Hausaufgabe werden an der Tafel gesammelt. Das Verhältnis des britischen Ehepaares zu den beiden Gastarbeitern, das sich von reiner Gastfreundschaft zu einer Eltern-Kind-Beziehung entwickelt, soll dabei im Mittelpunkt stehen.

Henry and Oxford

– a dozen Jamaicans were taken on at the motor works – he invited them to the flat – they meet all of Lou's and Raymond's friends – they come frequently	<u>friends</u> ⇓ <u>family</u>

Der heilen „Familie“ Lou – Raymond – Henry soll im Verlauf der Stunde die sich am Rande des Existenzminimums bewegende Familie von Lous Schwester Elizabeth gegenübergestellt werden. Zu diesem Zweck wird das bereits bearbeitete *Worksheet 17* um Informationen aus Elizabeths Leben ergänzt.

Read p. 99, l. 39 – p. 101, l. 40. Fill in the grid for Elizabeth.

	Lou and Raymond	Elizabeth
hometown	– Whitney Clay	– London
house	– new council house – block of flats	
flat	– fifth floor – three-roomed flat	– shabby ground-floor rooms
jobs	– Lou: used to be a nurse – Raymond:foreman at the motor works	– does not work
married life	– no children – married for quite a while	– eight children – single parent
pastimes	– reading (magazines, books) – no TV – rarely go to the cinema	
religion	– Catholic – take an active interest in their congregation – members of church committees	– Catholic
friend	– choose their friends carefully	

Im Unterrichtsgespräch werden zunächst diese Kriterien verglichen und die Unterschiede versprachlicht. Als ein Teil der Hausarbeit sollen die Ergebnisse schriftlich formuliert werden:

Use our results to write a text on the topic: The Life of Lou and Raymond in comparison with Elizabeth's lot *(Los)*. That is the first part of your homework.

The life of Lou and Raymond in comparison with Elizabeth's lot
Lou and Raymond live in a new industrial town in Britain in a three-roomed council flat on the fifth floor. As they have no children, they think this flat is just the right size for them. The fact that they have no children also enables them to lead an almost middle-class way of life, something they couldn't have afforded otherwise. Raymond works as a foreman in a factory, so he doesn't earn too much money and Lou has given up her job as a nurse. They read good books, but do not watch TV; they seem to be very conscious of the "do's and don'ts" of middle-class society. They are Catholics and are members of various church groups. They choose their friends who are either people from their congregation or from Raymond's factory, carefully. Lou and Raymond are well on their way up into the middle class.
Elizabeth, on the other hand, lives at the bottom of the social scale. She lives in a shabby flat in a bad area of London. As a single parent with eight children, she does not have time to work and so she has to rely on social benefits for the maintainance af her family. Elizabeth is also a Catholic but her faith doesn't seem to play a very big part in her life.

Der zweite Teil der Hausaufgabe dient der Vorbereitung zur nächsten Stunde, in der es um das Phänomen des „Wunders" der schwarzen Madonna gehen soll.

The second task for homework is: Scan the text for all information on the Black Madonna.

3.3 Religion and miracles

Die in der vorangegangenen Stunde erteilte schriftliche Hausarbeit wird nicht ausführlich thematisiert, da sie inhaltlich nur wiederholenden Charakter hat. Sie diente der Übung im schriftlichen Ausformulieren des mündlich geleisteten Vergleichs. Es ist empfehlenswert, mehrere Schülerarbeiten einzusammeln und korrigiert zurückzugeben.

Zum Einstieg sollen sich die Schülerinnen und Schüler mit dem Phänomen „Wunder" beschäftigen.

Do you believe in miracles? Have you ever witnessed or heard of a miracle come true?

Aus konkreten Beispielen soll die Wirkungsweise von Heiligenwundern abstrahiert und in einem nächsten Schritt anhand der Beispiele von Lous Gebeten für Henry und Oxford verifiziert werden.

Deduct the mechanism of miracles from your examples and verify it using the examples of Lou's prayers for Henry and Oxford. Leave some space for a third prayer which we will fill in later.

The working of miracles

negative situation	⇒	prayer	⇒	positive situation
1. Henry does not believe				Henry falls ill and regains his faith
2. Lou does not want Oxford to be near her				Oxford leaves for Manchester
3. Lou has no child				Lou has a black baby

Lous eigene Erfahrungen sowie Berichte in einer kirchlichen Zeitschrift veranlassen sie, für ein eigenes Kind zu beten. Den Komplex „Lou's baby" sollen die Schülerinnen und Schüler in Gruppenarbeit selbst erarbeiten.

Work in groups of four. It is up to you to organise your group and your groupwork in an efficient way. Scan the text from p. 107, l. 4–p. 111, l. 20 for information on the baby and then present the information in a mindmap.

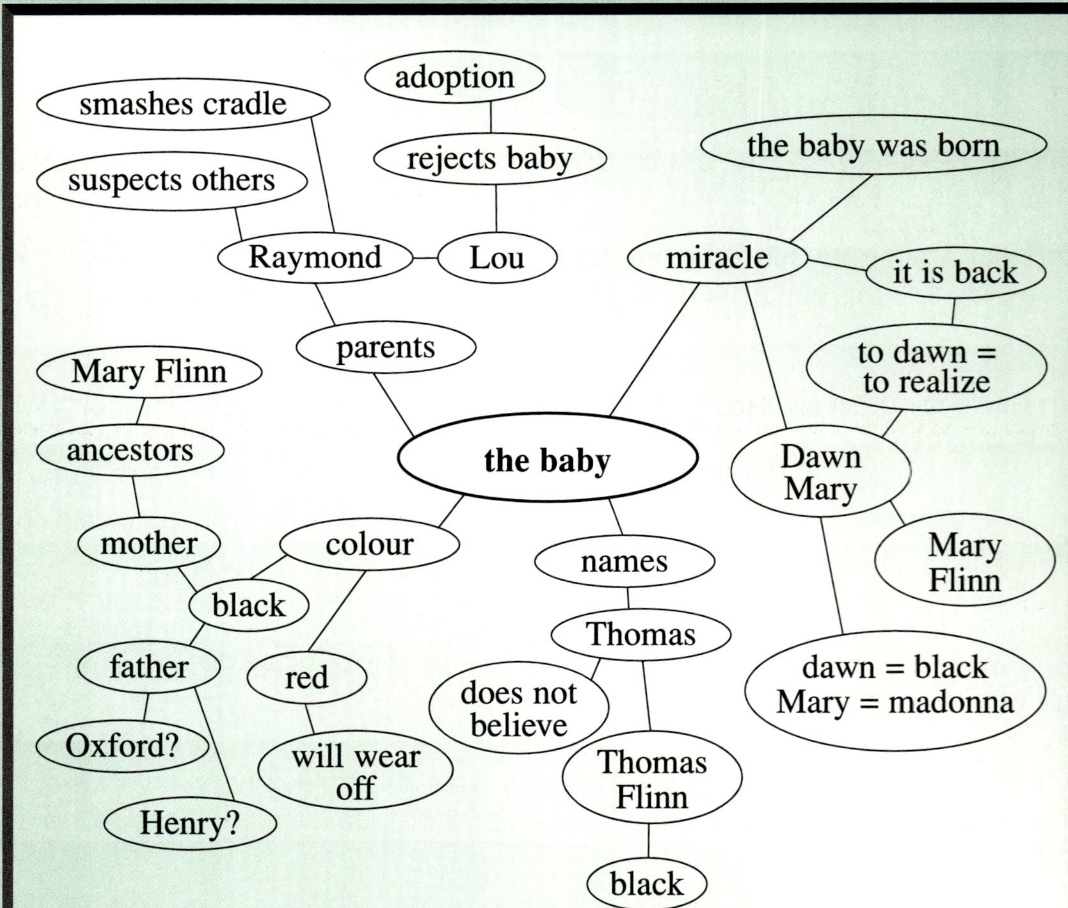

Die Gruppen halten ihre Mind-Maps auf Folien fest und stellen diese erklärend vor. Alle Schülerinnen und Schüler ergänzen dabei ihre Sammlungen und nutzen diese für die Erledigung der kreativen schriftlichen Hausarbeit.

Write a newspaper article on Lou's baby for a yellow press paper.

Black Baby Born to White Parents – the Black Madonna: Blessing or Curse?
Lou and Raymond Miller of Whitney Clay led a quiet life and were respected by their neighbours and loved by their friends. They had everything they could wish for, everything but a little baby to protect and love. After years of disappointing medical treatments, they had given up hope for a little family of their own and devoted themselves to their work in their congregation. But then everything changed, and there seemed to be new hope to make their dream of a family come true. Lou, herself, had experienced the miraculous powers of the Black Madonna of Whitney Clay on other occasions, so she decided to pray for a baby, and amazingly her prayers were heard by the Madonna. Lou became pregnant, and she and her husband Raymond were happier than ever. But what a shock when they saw their little baby for the first time! It was black! "At first we thought this must have been a terrible mistake, but then we got the results of the blood tests." Raymond Miller says.
Can this really be the workings of God? What is the secret of the Black Madonna? Our reporters found out that the statue had been cut from a piece of wood that was found in a bog in Ireland. Bogs are the places where, in ancient times, people deposited the bodies of criminals. Has one of the black souls from centuries past returned in the shape of the Black Madonna? We will continue our investigations and keep you informed.

3.4 The Black Madonna

Zum Abschluss der Interpretationsarbeit sollen sich die Schülerinnen und Schüler anhand von Lous und Raymonds Ehe noch einmal das Wirken der Black Madonna vergegenwärtigen. Dabei kann folgendes Tafelbild gemeinsam entwickelt werden:

Describe the influence of the Black Madonna on Lou's and Raymond's married life.

The influence of the Black Madonna

ordered life
⇓
– Henry and Oxford
– like a family with black "children"
– the "children" are cast out
⇓
the Black Madonna
⇓
– the baby
– a family with a black baby
– the baby is given away
⇓
disordered life

Have another look at what we found out about the workings of miracles and add Lou's third prayer.

negative situation	⇒	prayer	⇒	positive situation
[1. – 2. bereits ausgefüllt]				
3) Lou has no child				Lou has a black baby

Das Wirken der Black Madonna soll nun noch einmal unter der Fragestellung thematisiert werden, ob sie wirklich das gibt, was die Menschen von ihr erwarten und wie man mit unerwünschten Veränderungen im Leben umzugehen hat.
Dabei sollte auch Raymonds und Lous Rassismus thematisiert werden. Zwar erlaubt er es ihnen, sich im Sinne christlicher Tradition um zwei Einwanderer zu kümmern, aber trotz ihrer Verankerung in eben diesen christlichen Traditionen, verbietet er es ihnen, ihr eigenes – schwarzes – Kind anzunehmen. Der Unterschied zwischen rational richtigem Handeln (*doing the right thing* S. 111, Z. 14) und moralisch richtigem Handeln (*doing the good thing*, S. 111, Z. 18) soll erarbeitet werden.

How should people deal with undesirable changes in their lives: what is the difference between "doing the good thing" and "doing the right thing"?

Diese Diskussion leitet über zur Abschlussphase der Interpretationsarbeit. Lou und Raymond stellen sich auf dem *hot seat* den Fragen des Plenums und verteidigen ihre Entscheidung, das Kind zur Adoption freizugeben. [Zur Durchführung eines *hot seat* siehe Schallhorn/Peschel: *Method Guide*. Paderborn: Schöningh 2004, S. 67ff.]

Nach dieser kreativen Umsetzung des Inhaltes der Geschichte und wichtiger Handlungsmotive ergibt sich die Frage nach der Besonderheit der Kurzgeschichte. Die Schülerinnen und Schüler sollten erkennen, dass es sich um eine Satire handelt.

Notizen:

Qaisra Shahraz, *A Pair of Jeans* (1988/2004)

Die Autorin Quaisra Shahraz veröffentlichte zunächst im Jahre 1988 eine kürzere Version ihrer Erzählung *A Pair of Jeans*, die sie dann im Jahre 2004 in einer überarbeiteten Fassung noch einmal auf den Markt brachte. Die neue Fassung unterscheidet sich von der alten vor allem dadurch, dass vieles, was bisher nur angedeutet wurde, nun explizit dargestellt und erläutert wird, weshalb die Intention der Autorin klarer zum Ausdruck kommt. Sowohl die alte als auch die neue Fassung beinhalten zwei Schlussvarianten.

3.5 Identity

Wie der Titel der *short story* andeutet, stehen die Jeans der Hauptperson im Mittelpunkt der Erzählung. Dabei handelt es sich jedoch nicht einfach um ein Kleidungsstück, sondern um den Ausdruck einer ganzen Lebensphilosophie. Die Schülerinnen und Schüler sollen sich zunächst über die Bedeutung der Jeans in unserer Gesellschaft klar werden.
Zum Einstieg in die Arbeitsphase wird zunächst die Anzahl derjenigen Schülerinnen und Schüler ermittelt, die am betreffenden Unterrichtstag Jeans tragen. Da die Zahl erfahrungsgemäß sehr hoch sein wird, lässt es sich leicht zur Eingangsfrage überleiten.

What comes to your mind when you hear the word "jeans"?

Die Stichworte werden im Anschluss in einer Mind-Map an der Tafel organisiert.

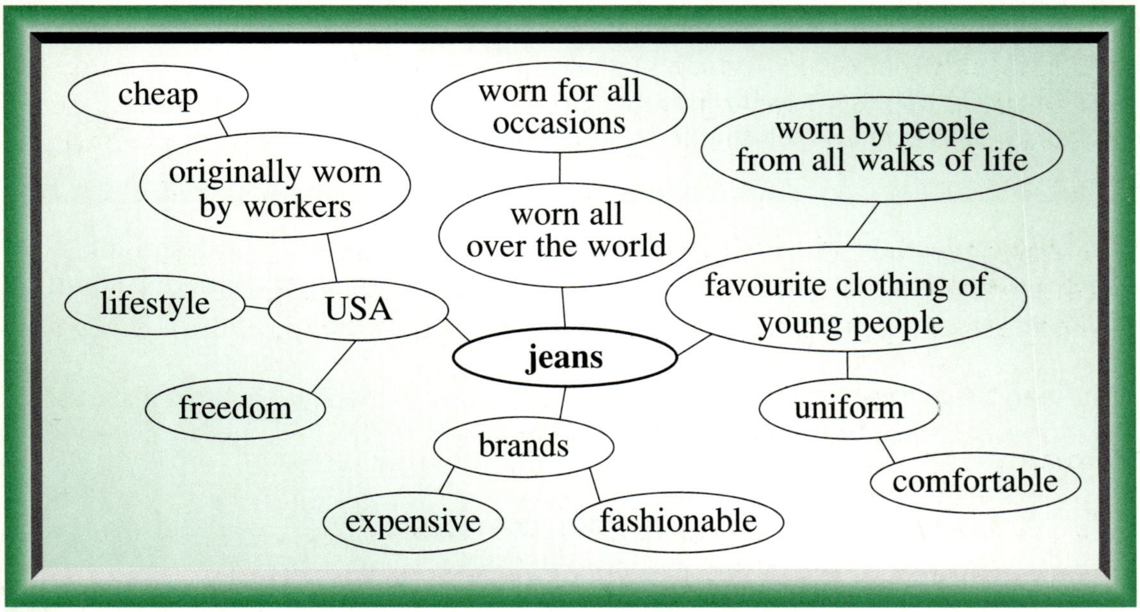

Im weiteren Unterrichtsgespräch sollen die Schülerinnen und Schüler die Bedeutung von Kleidung im Zusammenhang mit bestimmten Ereignissen und Situationen erkennen und diskutieren. Folgende Hilfsfragen können das Gespräch unterstützen:

- Are there special clothes for special occasions?
- Do you accept dress codes?
- What are their positive/negative aspects?
- What do we express by the way we dress?

Die letzte Hilfsfrage dient als Überleitung zur eigentlichen Erzählung. Dabei soll deutlich werden, dass Kleidung zum einen Individualität, zum anderen aber auch Zugehörigkeit zu einer bestimmten Gruppe zum Ausdruck bringen kann.

What does Miriam express through her clothes?

She belongs to a certain group: public
- western college girl – ~~outside~~ appearance/life
- Asian daughter – private life

In Partnerarbeit soll die Lerngruppe dies am Text belegen.

Work with your partner. Find examples in the text where we see Miriam, the western college girl, and Miriam, the Indian daughter (p. 111, l. 21 – p. 115, l. 8).

Die Ergebnisse der Partnerarbeit werden in einem Tafelbild festgehalten.

The two sides of Miriam

Miriam

<u>western college girl</u>	<u>Asian daughter</u> good
– jeans, short vest	– feels ~~odd~~ in her clothing
– midriff is visible	– conscious of her appearance
– western version of Miriam	– wants to put on different clothes
– discontent	– nervous
– rebellious	– her clothes burn her
– the same Miriam	– wears Indian clothes
– western fashion	– in control of herself
– western values	– plays the role of a demure bride

⇓

"Or was she the same person?" (p. 114, l. 48)
"Perhaps it was true that there were two sides to her character." (p. 115, ll. 1f.)

Die Lerngruppe soll in häuslicher Vorbereitung den Text zu Ende lesen und Passagen unterstreichen, die Miriams Unzufriedenheit mit ihrer Situation deutlich machen.

Read the whole text and underline the passages that show Miriam's dissatisfaction with her present situation.

3.6 A wanderer between two worlds

Die Schülerinnen und Schüler sollen sich noch einmal mit Miriams schwieriger Situation als *wanderer between two worlds* beschäftigen. Zunächst sollen die als Hausaufgabe ausgewählten Textpassagen als Grundlage für ein fiktives Gespräch dienen, das Miriam am nächsten Tag mit einer College-Freundin führt. Dieses Gespräch soll in Gruppen zu vier Schülern durchgeführt werden, wobei jeweils einer die Rolle der Miriam und ein anderer die Rolle ihrer Freundin übernimmt. Zwei Schüler dokumentieren das Gespräch, d.h. sie notieren die wichtigsten Argumente beider Seiten.

Work in groups of four. Imagine the following situation: The next day, Miriam talks with a British friend from college about what happened. We need one person to take the part of Miriam, another to take the part of her friend and two people to note down the most important arguments in the conversation.

Nach den Gruppengesprächen werden die wichtigsten Argumente an der Tafel gesammelt.

Miriam's problems

Miriam's problems ⟶	possible solutions
– Miriam is discontent	– Miriam should try to be herself
– Miriam wants to be seen as a person, not as a stereotype	– she should try to find a compromise between her two selves
– Miriam has no problems in combining two sets of values	– she should try to talk with her parents and her future in-laws and explain her position to them
– she hates her own hypocrisy	– Miriam should not give up one set of values completely for another, but try to combine them as far as possible
– she has to play roles to please others	

Miriams Situation wird noch einmal aufgegriffen. Die Liste der Vorschläge wird dabei auf ihre Realisierbarkeit überprüft.

3.7 The individual and society

In dieser Stunde soll die Rolle der Eltern im Leben von Miriam und Farook thematisiert werden. Als Einstieg wird ein kurzes Klassengespräch zum Thema „My parents and I" geführt. Grundlage für die Interpretationsarbeit ist das Gespräch zwischen den Schwiegereltern Begum und Ayub. Die Ergebnisse werden an der Tafel festgehalten.

The parents arranged the marriage of Miriam and Farook. What do Begum and Ayub fear from a daughter-in-law who is influenced by western forms of living? Collect keywords from their conversation (p. 116, l. 16 – p. 120, l. 39).

Miriam as a daughter-in-law:

- she is not modest
- she doesn't dress properly
- they cannot be proud of her
- she has the wrong friends
- she might have a bad influence on her in-laws' household
- she lives the life of an English college girl
- she wants to have personal freedom
- she might have a boyfriend or take drugs
- she might try to dominate her husband
- she is influenced by a western lifestyle

⇓

'I am sure we can find lots of other women for our son, women who have a more discreet taste in clothing and a good understanding of female modesty.'(p. 120, ll. 33-35)

Im anschließenden Unterrichtsgespräch soll die Haltung von Farooks Eltern als Intoleranz gegenüber der Lebensweise und dem Wertesystem der westlichen Gesellschaft entlarvt werden.

- Why do Ayub and Begum reject Miriam as a daughter-in-law?
- How do they see life in western society?
- What are their ideas of how a woman should look and behave?
- How do they try to protect their own value system?
- Is their reaction appropriate?
- What would you like to tell them?

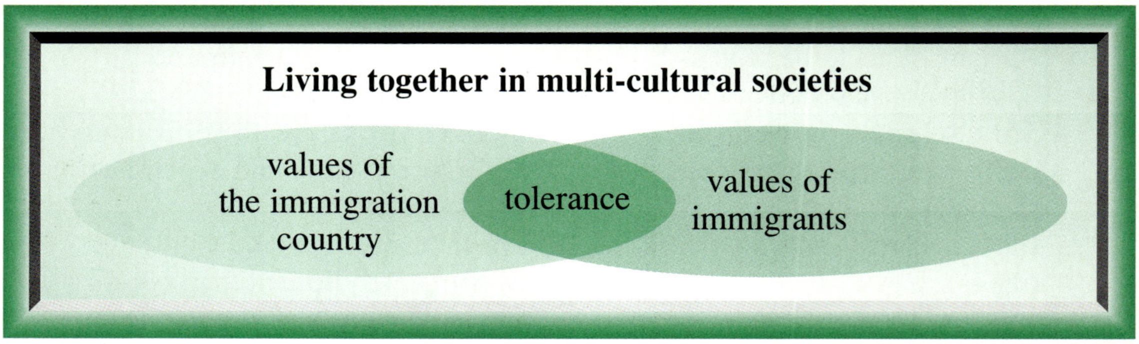

Zum Abschluss der Unterrichtseinheit sollen noch einmal alle angesprochenen Themen in einer Gesprächsrunde gebündelt werden. Miriam, Farook und ihre Eltern treffen sich zu einem Gespräch. Dieses kann in der Form einer *fishbowl* ablaufen.(Zur Methode der *fishbowl* siehe Schallhorn/Peschel, *Method Guide*, Paderborn, Schöningh: 2004)

Miriam, Farook, and their parents meet to talk about the situation. Discuss in fishbowl style.

Die Hausaufgabe greift die zwei von der Autorin angebotenen Schlussversionen der Geschichte auf:

Compare the two endings of the story and explain in writing which one you prefer.

Comparison of the two endings to Qaisra Shahraz, *A Pair of Jeans* (1988/ 2004)

I prefer the first ending because it is more in line with the Miriam we meet in the story. Miriam is a person who is torn between two worlds. She is aware of this situation and she suffers as a result of it but she cannot free herself from it. She is too involved in the traditions of her origins, which she also does not really reject. For this reason, she tries to satisfy the claims of both worlds, without firmly belonging to either. Had she been completely convinced of either the western or the eastern set of values, she would not have had any problems at all. This inner conflict makes Miriam insecure and vulnerable. All of this is visible in her symbolic act of pulling the pair of jeans from her wardrobe and kicking it with her foot. At this point, she is so disgusted by this – western – article of clothing that she cannot even touch it. Moreover, she blames the jeans for all the things that have recently gone wrong because she is not ready to see the fault in either herself or her fiancé's family.
The Miriam in the new ending is a very self-confident young woman who, in her decision to talk with her fiancé, disregards all the social rules that have hitherto determined her life. She is ready to make decisions and to live with the consequences. If the Miriam who felt so uncomfortable being caught in her scandalous western clothing at the beginning of the story turns into a self-confident, rebellious young woman overnight and takes her life into her own hands, then this is a very miraculous development indeed, but not a very convincing one.

Hanif Kureishi, *My Son the Fanatic* (1994)

Hinweis: Die *short story* wurde 1997 verfilmt. Das Unterrichtsmodell ist nur für die Arbeit mit dem Text konzipiert. Am Ende der Textarbeit bietet sich aber ein Vergleich mit der Verfilmung an.

3.8 Father-and-son relationship I (Parvez)

Es wird der Anfang der *short story* (S. 126, Z. 25–S. 127, Z. 17) entweder als Kopie oder im Lehrervortrag präsentiert. Dies ermöglicht, dass die Schülerinnen und Schüler darüber spekulieren, was mit Ali geschehen ist beziehungsweise geschieht.

What might be the case with Ali?

- Ali might need money
- Ali might be being blackmailed and need money
- Ali might be taking drugs and selling his things because he needs the money
- Ali might belong to a religious group which is against western-style luxury

“There are more important things to be done.” – What could this mean?

- Ali is preoccupied with something else
- Ali belongs to a political or religious group
- Ali belongs to a group that protects the environment, fights for human rights, etc.

Nun wird der Text mit den Schülerinnen und Schülern laut gelesen. Dabei erhalten sie den Auftrag, Passagen über Parvez und sein Leben in England zu unterstreichen.

We are going to read together from l. 18 on p. 127 to l. 20 on p. 129. Underline passages that give information on Parvez.

Es wird bis S. 129, Z. 20 („But he is growing a beard.“) gelesen und markiert. Danach werden die Informationen mündlich zusammengetragen:

p. 127:
- Parvez has been a taxi-driver for twenty years
- has worked for the same firm for ten years
- is a Punjabi
- avoids his wife
- the cabbies are his best friends
- lives as if he was still in Pakistan
- is proud and ashamed of talking about Ali’s behaviour to his friends
- likes to boast about Ali’s excellent school performance
- hopes for a good job for Ali
- wants him to marry the right girl and start a family
- his dream: doing well in England
- blames himself for having gone wrong in son’s upbringing

p. 128:
- Parvez has known Bettina, a prostitute, for three years
- they exchange private information like "soul-mates"
- Parvez is worried that Ali could be on drugs

p. 129:
- he observes Ali closely as a caring and worried father
- he feels criticised and reproached for something by his son but he cannot figure out what it is

Die so gewonnenen Informationen sollen nun in Partnerarbeit für das schriftliche Erstellen eines Personenprofils benutzt werden.

Work with your partner. Use the information you have found to write a profile of Parvez.

Parvez comes from the Pakistan state of Punjab. He has been a taxi-driver, a so-called "cabby", for twenty years. He is a very loyal person and does his job well for he has been employed by the same firm for the last ten years. Most of his friends are also Punjabi taxi-drivers. He lives with them as if he was still in Pakistan. He obviously does not strive for integration into British society. Parvez has one son, Ali, who he is very proud of. He likes to boast about his son's excellent school performance. When he finds out about Ali's strange behaviour, he is therefore ashamed of telling the others that his "perfect son" has left the right path. Ali is supposed to finally fulfil Parvez's dream of "doing well in England". Parvez certainly does not live the life of a pious Muslim. He tries to avoid his wife and has found a "soul-mate" in Bettina, a prostitute. He has been meeting with her for three years. She is the only person he can speak his mind to freely. When Ali starts behaving like a drug-addict, Parvez find's it very hard to understand his son's motives and blames himself for having done something wrong in his upbringing.

Schon hier zeichnet sich ab, dass Parvez das typische Leben eines Einwanderers der ersten Generation führt. Sein Lebensziel wird erst in der Karriere der zweiten Generation erfüllt. Dabei besteht gleichzeitig ein grundlegender Widerspruch zwischen diesem Wunschtraum des asiatischen Einwanderers und seinen muslimischen Traditionen. Dieses Dilemma wird im letzten Satz der Erzählung formuliert, jedoch auch hier nicht vom Autor aufgelöst. Nachdem einige Profile von der Lerngruppe vorgetragen und besprochen worden sind, wird die Lektüre mit lautem Lesen bis Seite 130, Zeile 15 fortgesetzt. An dieser Stelle wird nach den möglichen Gründen für Alis Weigerung, mit dem Vater eine Aussprache zu führen, gefragt. Die Schülerinnen und Schüler sollen aus den vorangegangen Hinweisen zu Alis „spirituellem Wandel“ argumentieren.

Why does Ali try to avoid a talk with his father?

Ali has now turned completely to religion. He knows that his father has a kind of trauma concerning praying as he was once ill-treated by his teacher, the maulvi, because he fell asleep during the prayers. Since then, Parvez has avoided religion, so Ali is sure his father would not understand his new way of life and therefore would only argue with him.

In der folgenden Stunde soll das Vater-Sohn-Verhältnis intensiver behandelt werden. Dazu wird der Auftrag gegeben, die Geschichte zu Hause fertig zu lesen und stichwortartige Notizen aus dem Text zum Verhältnis der beiden zu machen.

Finish reading at home. While reading, extract all information on the father-son-relationship and jot it down. Keywords and short notes will do.

3.9 Father-and-son relationship II (Parvez and Ali)

Am Anfang der Stunde sollen die Schülerinnen und Schüler kurz eine mündliche Inhaltsangabe des zu Hause gelesenen Textes geben:

What does Bettina learn from Parvez when he announces to her the next day: "I've just had the worst experience of my life." (p. 130, l. 27)?

Parvez muss sich von seinem Sohn für seine „dekadente" Lebensweise tadeln lassen. Sein Sohn ekelt sich vor ihm und hasst ihn (S. 131, Z. 6–7). Die moralische Verurteilung verursacht, dass Parvez im Restaurant einen Wutausbruch bekommt und einen Teller zu Boden wirft. Sein Sohn bleibt gleichmütig stur und wirft ihm vor, unzählige Male gegen den Koran verstoßen zu haben und zählt ihm seine „Sünden" auf (*eating pork, drinking alcohol, gambling etc*). Alis Hauptvorwurf verblüfft Parvez: „You are too implicated in Western civilisation" (S. 131, Z. 33–34). Parvez vergöttere die „Western materialists" und habe sich auf deren üble Werte eingelassen. Der Vater wird vom Sohn fanatisch belehrt, sodass er sich versichern muss, noch in London zu sein: „Parvez looked out the window as if to check that they were still in London." (S. 131, Z. 47–48)
Die Unterhaltung mit dem Sohn ist ein Schock für Parvez: „He knocked the side of the car [...] Parvez stumbled and fell in the road, scraping his hands and ripping his trousers." (S. 132, Z. 24–30) Ali sticht Parvez den Dolch ins Herz, als er verkündet sein Studium (*studies in accounting*) abzubrechen mit der Begründung: „Western education cultivates an anti-religious attitude" (S. 132, Z. 38–39). Sein neues Tätigkeitsfeld sei nun die Arbeit mit straffällig gewordenen Muslimen im Gefängnis. Parvez sieht seinen Sohn verloren und teilt Bettina mit, dass er Ali aus dem Haus werfen wird. (S. 133, Z. 1–6). Bettina besänftigt ihn und bringt ihn vorübergehend von der harten Maßnahme ab.

What happens after the conversation with Bettina? (p. 133, ll. 14f.)

For the next two weeks, Parvez shows real interest in Ali's beliefs and tries to talk sensibly with him. He even starts growing a beard. He tells Ali about his philosophy of life and that he expects respect from his son. The attempts Parvez makes are all in vain. Ali reacts like a religious fanatic and counters with ideological phrases and aggressiveness.

Die Lerngruppe soll erklären, warum Bettina zum Auslöser der väterlichen Gewalt gegen Ali wird:

What role does Bettina play in the relationship of the two?

Parvez loves her, although she is a prostitute. He depends on her as a caring and understanding partner. She wants him to be happy and that is why she tries to calm him about Ali. She even convinces Parvez not to throw Ali out of the house immediately but to take the trouble to talk things out with him. She knows how much he loves his son and wants the two to have a good relationship. When Ali behaves rudely to her, she is deeply hurt. He has hit her most sensitive point. Her reaction is that of panic and does not necessarily mean the end of her relationship with Parvez. Ali considers her as a whore, who has tempted his father into vice and thus he despises her. Parvez' violent outburst is caused by his son's disrespect and his fear of losing Bettina. He has suppressed his fury and anger about Ali up to that moment. The incident with Bettina is just the trigger that lets all of his frustration burst out. The beating of his son is an outlet for these emotions as well as an expression of desperate helplessness.

Mithilfe der Hausarbeit soll nun ein Schaubild zum Verhältnis der beiden angefertigt werden. Dazu sollen die Entwicklungsstufen in Partnerarbeit nachvollzogen und bearbeitet werden. Als gemeinsames Ergebnis kann folgendes Tafelbild entwickelt werden:

Work with your partner. Go through your notes and determine the different stages in the development of their relationship.

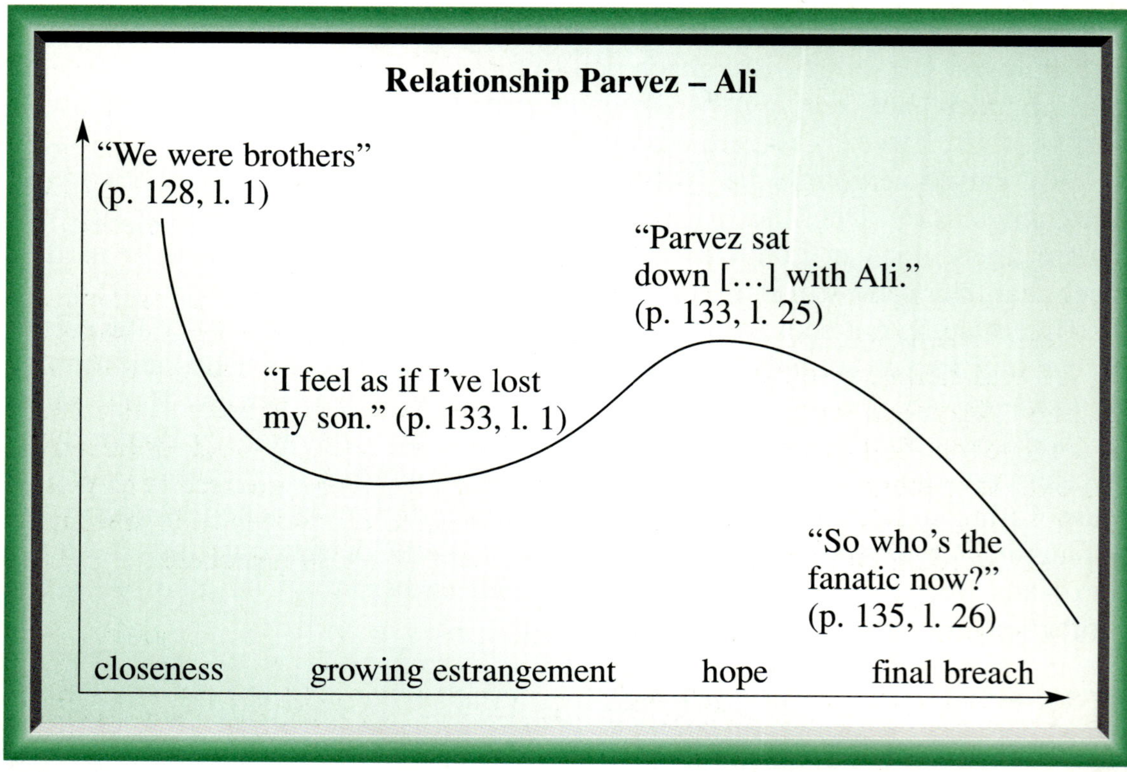

Für ein Rollenspiel in der nächsten Stunde soll die Lerngruppe zu Hause Textstellen suchen, in denen Ali sich über seinen Glauben äußert.

Scan the text for evidence of Ali's religious beliefs at home. Mark them with a pencil.

3.10 Interview with Ali, the fanatic

In dieser Stunde sollen die Schülerinnen und Schüler eine Pressekonferenz nachstellen, in der Alis religiöse Überzeugungen und seine daraus resultierenden Verhaltensweisen verdeutlicht werden. Zur Vorbereitung der Pressekonferenz sollen sich die Schülerinnen und Schüler zunächst über Alis Denkstrukturen klar werden. In einem zweiten Schritt werden Fragen für das Interview erarbeitet. Dazu werden zuerst die in der Hausarbeit markierten Stellen herangezogen.

Sum up your findings about Ali's beliefs in a short statement.

Ali's beliefs
Islam is the only true religion, and our aim is the worldwide rule of Islam. Our enemies are Christian and Jewish capitalists, who are exploiting the world. We will fight the adultery, homosexuality, drugs, prostitution and usury, which dominate western society. We will gladly give our lives in this fight because our reward will be paradise.

Als nächstes werden die Fragen vorbereitet:

Write down five questions each that you would like to ask Ali if you could meet him.

- When and how did you come into contact with your political and religious friends?
- What do you find most convincing in your political and religious views?
- What made you suddenly change your whole life?
- Did you find it hard to give up your western way of life?
- Which role did your father play in your personal development?

Let's stage a press conference in which one of you is Ali. We need five reporters. The others are observers. The observers note down the questions and take notes on the answers. Afterwards, we are going to evaluate the conference.

Ein Schüler oder eine Schülerin übernimmt die Rolle des Ali und platziert sich vor der Klasse. Nach dem Spiel werden die Agierenden zunächst nach ihrem Befinden befragt und nehmen selbst Stellung zu ihrer *performance*. Danach wird das gesamte Gespräch von den Beobachterinnen und Beobachtern inhaltlich wiedergegeben und nach Aussagegehalt, Überzeugungskraft und dergleichen beurteilt. Ausgehend von der Pressekonferenz soll nun die Frage nach dem Wesen von politischem und/oder religiösem Fanatismus gestellt und seine Mechanismen analysiert werden. Die Ergebnisse werden in einem Tafelbild gesichert.

Describe the mechanisms of political and/or religious fanaticism in general.

Reasons and function of fanaticism

dissatisfaction, boredom, disappointment,
meaninglessness in everyday life

⇓

religious or political ideology

⇓

complete devotion

⇓

convincing others (possibly by violent means)

Es bleibt zu erklären, warum Ali seinen Vater am Ende als Fanatiker bezeichnet.

How do you understand Ali's final remark: "So who's the fanatic now?"

Parvez verfolgt im Gunde ebenso fanatisch sein Ziel, aus Ali einen „guten“, erfolgreichen Engländer zu machen, wie Ali genau dies ablehnt. Dass Fanatismus in Gewalt münden kann, beweist Parvez’ Verhalten.
An dieser Stelle kann den Schülerinnen und Schülern die Information gegeben werden, dass Kureishi die Geschichte anlässlich der *fatwah* gegen Rushdie geschrieben hat.[1]

Kureishi wrote *My Son the Fanatic* in reaction to the Salman Rushdie affair. Can you imagine why?

The reaction to Salman Rushdie’s *The Satanic Verses* was ferocious, not only in strict Islamic countries but also in Islamic immigrant communities throughout Europe. Britain experienced severe uproar and raging crowds of fanatic Muslims. The incident brought a considerably large number of so-called “fundamentalists” to light and, as such to the attention of the public. Like Ali, lots of youngsters now living as the second generation in a country that is not their parents’ home country, have turned towards more radical forms of Islam. The reasons can be found in their search for identity in a society that does not truly integrate them. Treated as second class citizens, they suffer from discrimination and an existential lack of reliable values. They do not accept their parents as role models because they see that their parents are most often still the “underdogs” and are slaves to the materialistic cravings that they have fallen victim to in their new country. The younger generation has a problem with being brought up – on the one hand – in their traditional religion and witnessing – on the other hand – how decadently the older, more assimilated people behave. The rather strict religion appeals to those in search of stable rules and moral values. It is a retributive religion that promises that those living in sin will be duly punished. Those who cling to the Koran gain inner strength by joining together as a group. Their common belief gives them the security they cannot find in a society where everything seems to have dissolved into arbitrariness. In Ali’s case, his rejection of all opportunities, be they professional or purely pleasure, that goes along with his becoming more religious is simply an act of teenage rebellion against his father. His estrangement from the family is a clear indication of his frustration with what he experiences as the son of an immigrant.

Hier kann noch einmal auf Alis Reaktion auf Bettina eingegangen werden. Für ihn ist es offensichtlich so, dass sein Vater seine Mutter mit ihr betrügt. Die Mutter wird in der Geschichte kaum benannt. Vielmehr heißt es, dass Parvez seiner Ehefrau wie die anderen Pakistaner auch, lieber aus dem Weg geht (S. 127, Z. 25). Das lässt Rückschlüsse auf die Familiensituation zu. Hier schließt die kreative Hausarbeit an:

Ali leaves home but stays in close contact with his parents. He and his father exchange letters. Write either Ali’s letter to his father or Parvez’s letter to his son, explaining again their respective points of view.

C

Dear son,
I am writing this letter to you because I want you to understand why I lead my life the way I do. You know I came from a very poor part of Pakistan to England because I dreamed of a better life for me – and after you were born, for you, my son, as well. I’ve always worked hard and done everything I could to make sure

[1] Introduction: Hanif Kureishi: The Road Exactly. In: *My Son the Fanatic*, London: Faber and Faber, pp. VII–XII.

that you would be able to lead a better life than me. Perhaps I have forgotten about more important things in my desire to make my dreams come true. Perhaps I should have led a more pious life than I have done, but then, I have always tried to be a good man. Don't you think there are more important laws in the Koran than the ones about not eating pork or drinking alcohol? I've never harmed another person, I obey the law, I am honest and I have tried to be a good father and a loving husband.
I know I cannot make you come back home or resume your old way of life. Everyone has to find his own way and you have found yours. But Ali, please don't ever submit to cruelty or violence. If you want to lead a life of piety, then do so, but let others live the way they want to.
Your loving father

Notizen:

Salman Rushdie, *Good Advice is Rarer than Rubies* (1994)

3.11 Miss Rehana's emancipation

Der erste Teil der *short story* (S. 135, Z. 25 – S. 138, Z. 17) wird bei geschlossenen Büchern über CD präsentiert. Die Schülerinnen und Schüler sollen ein passendes Ende dazu schreiben. Es ist zu erwarten, dass Miss Rehana in den meisten Geschichten ihre Einreisegenehmigung nach Großbritannien erhalten wird.

Write the ending of the short story.

Ending to: Salman Rushdie, *Good Advice is Rarer than Rubies* (1994)
Rehana went into the British Consulate. Together with all the other women, she had to wait in a corridor. They were all sitting on a long, uncomfortable bench outside an office. One after the other, they were called in. The women looked nervous and hardly dared to whisper. All of them wanted to go to Britain, either to join members of their families, to get married or simply to look for a job. After what seemed an eternity, Rehana's name was shouted by an unfriendly guard. She went into the office and handed her papers to a very strict-looking British clerk. He checked them carefully. Rehana couldn't help thinking of the old man outside the gates. Perhaps she should have listened to him and bought the passport he had offered her. It would have saved her a lot of trouble. As he had predicted, the clerk asked her a lot of questions, some of which were difficult to answer. Rehana was never sure if she was saying the things she was expected to say. 'Why do you want to go to Britain?' 'Do you want to work there?' 'Is there anyone who can take care of you?' In the end, Rehana was quite exhausted, and she was afraid she hadn't done well during the interview. To her surprise, the clerk suddenly put a stamp on a piece of paper and handed it to her. 'You are permitted to emigrate to Great Britain. These are your papers.' Rehana was relieved. She ran out of the building to tell the old man the good news.

Im Anschluss an den Vortrag und die Besprechung einiger Schülerarbeiten wird das Ende der Geschichte über CD präsentiert. Die Lerngruppe kann nun mitlesen. Im Unterrichtsgespräch werden die Unterschiede zwischen dem, was die Schülerinnen und Schüler geschrieben haben, und dem tatsächlichen Erzählausgang thematisiert. Dabei soll deutlich werden, dass Rehana nicht dem erwarteten Rollenbild entspricht. Dies soll am Text belegt werden. Die Ergebnisse werden stichwortartig an der Tafel gesammelt:

Read p. 135, l. 38 – p. 136, l. 18 again. Underline passages in the text that give us information on the sort of women who usually wait in front of the British Consulate and on Miss Rehana.

The image of …

the Tuesday women	⇔	**Miss Rehana**
– frightened		– men are friendly to her
– some vested, a few barefaced		– barefaced
– come with male family members		– comes on her own
		– independent

Als Hausaufgabe soll Muhammad Alis Tätigkeit als „Berater" und sein verändertes Geschäftsgebaren in Bezug auf Miss Rehana untersucht werden.

Concentrate on the character of Muhammad Ali. What are the stages of his usual course of business. Where does he deviate from this course in his dealings with Miss Rehana?

3.12 Good advice

Die Hausaufgabe wird in Kleingruppen besprochen. Jeweils 4-6 Schülerinnen und Schüler ermitteln zunächst die beste Hausaufgabe ihrer Gruppe, ergänzen und korrigieren diese gegebenenfalls. Sie wird anschließend dem Plenum über Folie präsentiert. Im Unterrichtsgespräch soll geklärt werden, weshalb Muhammad Ali im Falle von Miss Rehana von seinem üblichen Geschäftsgebaren abweicht. Dabei soll deutlich werden, dass Muhammad Ali von der jungen, attraktiven Miss Rehana, die so anders ist als die Frauen, die er normalerweise kennen lernt, fasziniert ist.

Muhammad Ali – the businessman

1. he waits for inexperienced women who need an immigration permit for England
2. he offers his advice at a small cost

Miss Rehana gets advice for free

3. he helps the women to fill in their application forms, pretending to know a lot about Great Britain
4. he tells the women about the interview and makes them afraid of it
5. he offers the help of a "friend" who can obtain the necessary papers for another small fee

Miss Rehana is offered a passport

⇒ he is paid twice: 1. for his advice
2. for the faked papers

Es ergibt sich die Frage, was guter Rat im Allgemeinen und im Besonderen, d. h. für die „Tuesday women" und für Miss Rehana, bedeutet. Die textbezogenen Erklärungen werden an der Tafel notiert.

Coming back to the title: What really is "good advice" for Muhammad Ali and the Tuesday women, on the one hand, and for Miss Rehana, on the other hand?

Good advice

Muhammad Ali and the Tuesday women	Miss Rehana
"Go to England."	"Stay in India."
– people follow his advice	– Rehana doesn't follow his advice
– he earns a living	– she leads an independent life

⇓

"Good advice	is rarer than rubies"

Zum Abschluss der Interpretation sollen sich die Schülerinnen und Schüler in einer Kreativaufgabe noch einmal über das Außergewöhnliche an Miss Rehana klar werden. Dazu sollen sie in Partnerarbeit einen Dialog schreiben und diesen anschließend präsentieren.

Imagine the following situation: In the evening, Muhammad Ali meets a friend. He tells him about his experiences with Miss Rehana. Write a dialogue.

Dialogue between Ali and his friend Iqbal.

Ali: Hello, Iqbal, how are you, my friend?

I.: Fine, thanks Ali, but what's wrong with you? Why are you so upset? Sit down a moment and have a tea and some pakoras with me.

Ali: Pakoras … let me tell you about what is on my mind. I had a most unusual customer today. Normally, these Tuesday women are so glad to obtain my advice, but this woman I met today was completely different.

I.: Ah, come on, they are, all in all, just a bunch of stupid chickens who would be better off going home and serving their husbands as decency requires.

Ali: Yes, yes … but she was beautiful and absolutely fascinating.

I.: Ali, Ali, why, you old chum, have you fallen in love with this lady?

Ali: Go away – no – what an idea, me and the lass ... Listen, when I approached her and offered her my advice, she at first listened attentively but she wouldn't accept my help.

I.: I say, does this mean good old Ali has at last had a rejection? Who would have thought as much!

Ali: Well, I must say, I warned her about the embarrassing procedures they use to check the prospective immigrants and what kind of nasty questions they have to answer but before I could stop her, she marched straight into the British Consulate and – it all went wrong.

I.: Hm, poor lassie – but how come?

Ali: Just imagine – she gave all the wrong answers and what I still do not comprehend is that she was so very happy about failing the immigration test!

I.: What could be the reason for such foolish behaviour, Ali? Do you know anything about her reasons for emigrating to Great Britain?

Ali: Well, she told me she currently had a good job as a nanny for the sons of a rich family and that she had never seen the man her parents had chosen for her as a husband. He lives in Bradford, England and is a lot older than her. Her parents – oh, what misery would now be upon them if they knew that their daughter was not able to join the well-situated, prospective son-in-law – well "prospective" that is, if they had still been alive. You see, they arranged the marriage when she was still a child. Everything was planned so well … what a shame.

I.: Ali, has the idea ever occurred to you that she might have failed on purpose? She seems not to have had the slightest ambition to get to her betrothed. When you told her how to pass the examination and what she mustn't do, you of course made her aware of what to do in order to be sent away. So she played the idiot girl and got what she wanted: a very good excuse for not entering Great Britain and avoiding the compulsory marriage.

Ali: Gosh, you are right, Iqbal. So she took my advice after all – but in her very own way … that clever Miss Rehana, what a lass! Let's have another tea and some more pakoras.

Weiterführende Literatur

Archer, Stanley: W. Somerset Maugham. A Study of the Short Fiction, New York, Texas A&M University Twayne Publishers, 1993

Fraser, Gail: Shorter Fiction, in: The Cambridge Companion to Joseph Conrad, ed. by J.H. Stape, Cambridge, Cambridge University Press, 1996, pp. 25 – 44

Holden, Philip: Orienting Masculinity, Orienting Nation. W. Somerset Maugham's Exotic Fiction, Westport, CT, Greenwood Press, 1996

Honeff, Sibylle: George Orwell und der englische Imperialismus, Dissertation Bonn, 1984

Kureishi, Hanif: The Road Exactly: Introduction to My Son the Fanatic, in: Dreaming and Scheming: Reflections on Writing and Politics, London, Faber & Faber, 2002, pp. 215 – 221

Levenson, Michael (ed.): The Cambridge Companion to Modernism, Cambridge, Cambridge University Press, 1999

Lothe, Jakob: Conrad's Narrative Method, Oxford, Clarendon Press, 1989

Mayers, Valerie: George Orwell, Basingstoke, Macmillan, 1991

Meyers, Jeffrey: Policing Burma 1922 – 1972, in: Orwell. Wintry Conscience of a Generation, New York, Norton o.J.

Schemann, Michael: Imperialismus im Werk George Orwells, Frankfurt am Main, Peter Lang, 1999

Thorpe, Michael: Doris Lessing's Africa, London, Evans, 1978

Wilson, Edmund: New Yorker 13. Jan. 1951, 76, in: George Orwell: The Critical Heritage, ed. by Jeffrey Meyers, London, Routledge & Kegan Paul, 1975

Internet

www.postcolonialweb.org

EINFACH ENGLISCH
Unterrichtsmodell
Joyce Carol Oates
Big Mouth & Ugly Girl
Schöningh